MW00818019

Start Small, Stay Small

A Developer's Guide to Launching a Startup

Written by Rob Walling

Edited by Mike Taber

Copyright © 2010 Rob Walling

www.startupbook.net

ISBN 978-0-615-37396-6

First Edition

For my Mom and Dad, who years ago taught

me the value of hard work.

Contents

Preface

Who is this Book For?

This book is aimed at developers who want to launch their startup with no outside funding. It's for companies started by real developers solving real pain points using desktop, web and mobile applications.

This book intentionally avoids topics restricted to venture-backed startups such as: honing your investor pitch, securing funding, and figuring out how to use the piles of cash investors keep placing in your lap.

In this book I assume:

- You don't have $6M of investor funds sitting in your bank account
- You're unable to relocate to the handful of startup hubs in the world
- You're unwilling to work 70 hour weeks for low pay with the hope of someday making millions from stock options

There's nothing wrong with pursuing venture funding and attempting to grow fast like eBay, Google, Twitter, and Facebook. It just so happens that most people are not in a position to pursue this option.

What Does This Book Cover?

The focus of this book is building and launching a successful software, web or mobile startup with no external funding.

This process includes:

- Developing the proper mindset for a self-funded startup
- Understanding the Market-First Approach
- Finding and testing a niche market
- Choosing the optimal platform, price and revenue model
- Building a killer sales website
- Understanding the primary purpose of your sales website
- Building the right kind of interest, and thus driving the right kind of traffic, to your website
- Learning how to outsource
- Working with virtual assistants
- Determining what to do after launch: do you grow the business or start over?

If you're reading this book I assume you are an experienced software developer, so we won't be covering the development process. If you need assistance building software there are books written with that purpose in mind.

As I began the writing process, I received input from developers who told me they were tired of "filler" material – weak case studies, superficial interviews, chapters describing 10 options for how to accomplish a task but no guidance on which path to take or how to decide between them.

So I've focused on providing a practical, step-by-step approach to getting your startup off the ground and focused on making every word count. No filler allowed.

If you aren't frantically underlining, highlighting or taking notes as you read each chapter, I have not achieved my goal for this book.

To ask a question, make a comment or purchase the print, ebook or audio version of this book, visit www.StartupBook.net

About the Author

One question that should be on your mind as you start reading any book is: why should I listen to this author? Here is my track record so far.

My day job is managing 10 profitable software products and websites that I've built or acquired over the past ten years. I blog about startups, online marketing, and software and web entrepreneurship at www.SoftwareByRob.com.

And with my colleague Mike Taber, I run an online startup community with several hundred members called the Micropreneur Academy.

About the Micropreneur Academy

The Micropreneur Academy is a paid online learning environment and community website for startup founders.

Although this book contains a small amount of material from the Micropreneur Academy, it only covers topics that are conducive to the printed page.

The purpose of the Micropreneur Academy is to present topics that require interactive elements (screencasts, audio, and worksheets), topics that change frequently, cutting-edge approaches and our complete Rolodex of vendors and contractors. In addition it provides a community of like-minded startup founders accessible via private forums.

If you are interested in launching or growing your startup faster, as an owner of this book you are entitled to the first month of the Academy at no charge. To receive your free month visit www.Micropreneur.com/book/

And with that...let's get started.

Chapter 1

The Chasm Between Developer and Entrepreneur

What is an Entrepreneur?

An entrepreneur is a visionary

He is the person who sees the potential in an idea and creates a viable business from nothing.

She is the person who invests hundreds of hours into building, launching and marketing a product, fighting through every roadblock along the way.

In this book we'll cover the approaches of two types of entrepreneurs:

- **Micropreneurs** – Entrepreneurs who want to remain solo. This means no employees under any circumstance. Micropreneurs might own a single product, or may own many products that collectively contribute to their bottom line. A specific lifestyle is the goal of a Micropreneur.
- **Bootstrappers** – A bootstrapper has their vision set on something larger than a single person venture. Perhaps

5 employees, perhaps 10...a bootstrapper has an idea and knows she must execute and grow her company to survive.

It so happens that 90% of the knowledge needed to succeed at Micropreneurship and bootstrapping is identical. Finding a niche, finding a product, building, launching, marketing...it's the same process.

In this book I will point out a handful of places where the two paths diverge and call out the recommended approach based on the path you're following.

Why the Anti-Venture Capital Stance?

I wanted to address this early so you're clear on the focus of this book.

I am not anti-venture capital. I am anti-everyone-thinking-venture-capital-is-the-only-way-to-start-a-tech-company.

Seeking funding of any kind creates two problems.

First, it involves a massive investment of time and focus, which distracts you from the important things, like making money and staying in business.

Second, it makes modest success nearly impossible due to the limits it places on the potential markets you can pursue.

If you're self-funded with one or two founders, you can support your entire business from a tiny niche that provides $10k/month in revenue.

But with venture capital (or even a few hundred thousand in angel funding) you are forced to go after much larger markets. And a market that's 10x the size is 100x harder to get right. There's more competition, more complexity, higher advertising rates, more SEO competition, and a more fragmented audience.

Targeting a large, non-niche market is expensive in terms of marketing and support. It will eat you alive if you tackle it from the start.

But if you start small and make a product so good that your niche is falling all over itself to sign up, word will spread and you will soon find yourself with a product that extends beyond your tiny niche.

However, this takes time to grow organically; an approach that outside funding does not allow.

A Look at the Self-Funded Startup Entrepreneur

There are many definitions of entrepreneur, but since we'll be discussing self-funded tech startups we are going to focus our definition on a few key points:

Point 1: An entrepreneur is a technical visionary who creates software for a niche market.

Niche markets are critical. If you want to self-fund a startup you have to choose a niche.

Building an online invoicing software as a service (SaaS) application? Good luck.

Building an online invoicing application targeted at landscape architects? Now you're talking.

The genius of niches is they are too small for large competitors, allowing a nimble entrepreneur the breathing room to focus on an underserved audience. Once you've succeeded in that niche, you can leverage your success to establish credibility for your business to move into larger markets.

Point 2: An entrepreneur merges existing technical knowledge with online marketing knowledge.

The key factor in an entrepreneur's success is their ability to market their product. I can almost hear you groaning...but keep an open mind. Millions of people in this world can build software. A fractional subset of those can build software *and* convince people to buy it.

A developer who knows how to market a product is a rare (and powerful) combination.

Point 3: An entrepreneur is a cross between a developer, a webmaster, and a marketer.

Developer

Software entrepreneurship would be nearly impossible without the technical skills we learn as developers. The ability to fix a production site that's crashing or put together a hot fix for a key customer will be critical to your success.

Webmaster

These days it's imperative that your startup knows how to sell online. This means creating a website that converts visitors into customers. We'll be exploring a number of ways to build high-converting sales websites, and doing these will require basic HTML knowledge.

Once your website is up, you will be making constant updates, adding new content to achieve better search engine rankings, tweaking conversions (newsletter sign-ups, trials, purchases, etc...) and most of these tasks will be better executed if you can make small changes yourself. Basic knowledge of HTML or a CMS is essential.

Marketer

Marketing is more important than your product.

Let me say it another way:

> *Product Last. Marketing First.*

Your product has to be good. If it's not, you'll be out of business.

But before you build a good product you have to find your market. With an enormous amount of anecdotes to back me up I strongly believe that building something no one wants is the most common source of failure for entrepreneurs.

In chapter 2 we'll look at how to make sure people want what you're building *before* you build it.

Self-funded vs. Venture-funded

Self-funding your startup is worlds apart from what most people talk about in the tech startup world.

Venture-backed startups typically raise capital from outside investors with the goal of massive, accelerated growth. They attack large, growing markets with the hopes of 100x growth in 5 years or less.

Examples abound, but think along the lines of Netscape, Google, Travelocity, Yelp, Twitter and Facebook. Big dollars. Fast growth. High risk.

If you're a venture-backed startup founder you're looking at many years of long hours with a small potential for a huge payoff.

A bootstrapper still seeks growth, but at a slower pace since they do it organically through the re-investment of profit. They focus on smaller markets or niches within larger markets and grow both profit and headcount organically.

Examples include Joel Spolsky's Fog Creek Software and Eric Sink's SourceGear. Keywords: slower growth, less risk.

If you're a self-funded startup founder, you're looking at a decent potential for a decent payoff.

A Micropreneur has goals that are not limited to financial gain and more often involve lifestyle goals. Being able to live where you want and work when you want is an appealing option for many founders.

Two Real-life Examples

A Micropreneur: Ruben Gamez

Ruben Gamez is a Micropreneur. He has a full-time job as a development manager, but launched his SaaS application Bidsketch[1] in 2009. Today, he makes a tidy monthly income from this application. Ruben has no plans to leave his job, but enjoys the extra income, the control he can exert over his own project, and the experience of learning how to build, launch and market his own application.

The lessons Ruben has learned over the past year of launching and growing Bidsketch will apply to his future efforts, and he plans to launch other products during the coming year. His long-term goal is serial Micropreneurship and eventually, self-employment.

A Bootstrapper: Harry Hollander

Harry started Moraware Software[2] with a business partner. Their goal was to provide scheduling software for countertop installers, and within six months they knew it was a viable business. Eight years later Moraware employs four people in

---

[1] www.bidsketch.com

[2] www.moraware.com

addition to the two founders, all of whom work virtually from their respective homes.

Moraware focuses on the construction vertical niche and more specifically, countertop contractors. Limiting themselves to this group of people has a lot to do with their success. They've been able to focus on filling the exact needs of their customers and as a result they own a large portion of the countertop scheduling software market.

Starting for the Right Reasons

Most developers want to build software products for the wrong reasons.

Reason #1: Having a Product Idea

If you have an idea for a product, odds are high that you have *project/product confusion*.

A *project* is a software application that you build as a fun side project. The code is fun to write because you're not concerned about quality and performance, and the end result is a neat little application that likely isn't of use to many people.

A *product* is a project that people will pay money for. In other words, it's a project that has a *market* (a group of people who want to buy it). Without a market, a software application is just a project.

Most developers who come up with an idea know exactly how they will build it, but no idea how they will reach potential customers. They think a link from TechCrunch will drive hundreds, if not thousands, of sales.

On rare occasions the product-first approach works, but for the most part it's a recipe for failure.

Reason #2: To Get Rich

Getting rich shouldn't be your goal when launching a product.

Thousands of people with significantly more coding and marketing skills have built and launched products, yet still work for a living. If you are doing it for the money you will not stick around during those long months of hard work when no money is coming in.

If you want to make a million dollars, buy a lottery ticket or start a venture-backed startup; the odds of succeeding at either are very much not in your favor, but the potential payout is big.

As I said earlier, I'm pretty sure you're here to do something with less risk and less reward, but a much higher chance for success. A million dollar payday is most likely not in your future, but owning a successful startup can be.

Reason #3: Because It Sounds Like Fun

We've all read the stories of a successful startup and dreamed that we would one day be that person in the *Fast Company* article. Whether it's someone who hits it big with a fluke Facebook application or works for years to build a successful software company that you've followed through their blog, the story is always romanticized. In other words, the few glimpses you have into the life of a startup are not a true indication of what goes on behind the scenes to make it work.

If you want to become a Micropreneur because it *sounds like fun,* you're going to have a rude awakening on the 10th day when the initial excitement has worn off and you're slogging through exception handling code at one in the morning.

To throw more fuel on the fire, what you know about software development is a small piece of the puzzle. Writing code, where most of us are well-versed, is only about 30% of the work needed to launch a successful product.

The other 70% is debugging, optimizing, creating an installer, writing documentation, building a sales website, opening a merchant account, advertising, promoting, processing sales, providing support, and a hundred other things we'll dive into in later modules. Some of it is great fun...other parts, not so much.

Suffice to say that being an entrepreneur can be fun, but the fun parts come only with hundreds of hours of hard work.

What are the Right Reasons?

The "right" reason to start a startup depends on your goals. As I mentioned before, Micropreneurs lean towards lifestyle choices (freedom, income independence, location independence), while bootstrappers might embrace the challenge and excitement of owning their own business, to build equity in something they own, and to have control over the projects they work on.

Paying the Price of Success

Software entrepreneurship is a fantastic experience. The first time someone pays you for software you wrote, your head will nearly spin off its axis.

And ultimately, if you're able to harness the power of leveraging software instead of time, you can achieve more freedom than you're ready for. The first time I took a one month vacation I had the nagging feeling that I needed to do 160 hours of work when I got home...then I realized that hours and dollars no longer correlated.

It's hard to re-train your mind out of the dollars-for-hours mentality. For me it took well over a year.

The price to achieve this kind of payoff involves a huge up-front investment of time.

Or it may involve a substantial financial investment acquiring products.

Or maybe you'll decide to step away from the code, give up that control we all feel we need, and hire out some development so you focus on other areas of the business.

The price you pay is negotiable and is truly guided by your personal goals. But the bottom line is: you will have to pay a price.

It's a long road to becoming a successful entrepreneur. There will be many long nights, especially in the beginning. It's critical to know what you want out of entrepreneurship so you can make the right decisions along the way, and to give you something to hold onto when you're burning the midnight oil for the fifteenth night in a row.

What Are Your Goals?

Knowing your goals will allow you to make the right decisions as you start (or continue on) your path through entrepreneurship.

People start startups for a plethora of reasons, both personal and professional. Hard decisions lie ahead and the answers depend on what you want to get out of your startup experience.

As an example, which of the following sounds most appealing?

1. Keeping your day job and earning extra money on the side.
2. Building a portfolio of products and quitting your day job while still writing code.
3. Quitting your day job with the intent of outsourcing the code and focusing on the entrepreneurial side.
4. Quitting your day job and running a small company where you work from home and may have a few employees.

There are other options, of course, but your answer to the above depends on your personal preferences, desires and time constraints. Luckily you don't have to decide everything now.

But it's good to begin thinking about your motivation for starting a startup because it dictates the type of product you should launch.

The Power of Goals

To nail down what you want out of entrepreneurship, you need to decide on your goals. This is a process most people skip due to skepticism about the benefits of the process.

A study at Dominican University[3] revealed that the following 3 factors substantially increased someone's chance of following through on their goals:

1. **Written Goals** – "Those who wrote their goals accomplished significantly more than those who did not write their goals."
2. **Public Commitment** - "...those who sent their commitments to a friend accomplished significantly more than those who wrote action commitments or did not write their goals."
3. **Accountability** – "...those who sent weekly progress reports to their friend accomplished significantly more than those who had unwritten goals..."

It may feel like you're an exception; that you don't need goals or accountability...but trust the science and give it a shot. Spend 20 minutes making a list of the things you are hoping to accomplish by starting up. If you believe what was said above, it will make a big difference. Worst case, you waste 20 minutes of your time.

Remember that there is no single *best* path to success as a startup founder. Since you are deciding on a specific lifestyle and are making sacrifices to get there, it can look like almost anything. Just be sure it's what you want.

---

[3] Summary of Recent Goals Research, by Gail Matthews, Ph.D., Dominican University

The second two items, public commitment and accountability, can be achieved by interacting with a community of like-minded startup founders. You can find this through local Meetup groups[4], or through an online community like the Micropreneur Academy[5].

In the Academy, we have an accountability room where founders post weekly updates on their progress and discuss roadblocks that are impacting their progress because we know that it does help people to achieve their goals.

One Short-Term Goal I Propose
Here's one question you should think about right now: what is a good short-term goal for your startup?

I have a suggestion to help get you started:

> *Strive to build a startup that generates $500 per month in profit.*

This may sound like an easy goal, but will require more work than you can fathom at this point.

Once you've done that you will have so much experience under your belt you won't believe how much you know (and how little you knew when you started).

The Dip (a.k.a. The Software Product Myth)
The reason you need goals and accountability is to stay motivated during the hard times. Without goals you are much more likely to throw in the towel when things get difficult. This might be when you launch and no one buys, or you are

---

[4] www.meetup.com

[5] www.micropreneur.com

bombarded with so many support requests you don't have enough time to build new features.

Most developers start as salaried employees, slogging through code and loving it because they never imagined a job could be challenging, educational, and downright fun. Where else can you learn new things every day, play around with computers, and get paid for it?

A certain percentage of developers become unhappy with salaried development over time (typically it's shortly after they're asked to manage people, or maintain legacy code), and they dream of breaking out of the cube walls and running their own show. Some choose consulting, but many inevitably decide to build a software product.

"After all," they think "you code it once and sell it a thousand times – it's like printing your own money! I build apps all the time, how hard could it be to launch a product?"

Against All Odds

Most often the developer who chooses to become a consultant (whether as a freelancer or working for a company), does okay. She doesn't have a ton of risk and gets paid for the hours she works.

But developers who make the leap to their own startup are another story. Building a product involves a large up-front time investment, and as a result is far riskier than becoming a consultant because you have to wait months to find out if your effort will generate revenue. In addition, growing a product to the point of providing substantial income is a long, arduous road.

But let's say, for the sake of argument, that you spend 6 months of your spare time and you now own a web-based car key locator that sells 100 copies per month at $25 a pop. At long last, after months of working nights and weekends, spending every waking moment poring over your code, marketing, selling, and burning the midnight oil, you're living the dream of owning your own startup.

Except for one thing.

Support is Brutal

In our scenario you're now making $2500/month from your product, but since you make $60k as a salaried developer, you're not going to move back in with your parents so you can quit your day job.

So you work 8-10 hours during the day writing code for someone else, and come home each night to a slow but steady stream of support emails. The worst part is that if you've built your software right the majority of the issues will not be problems with your product, but degraded OS installations, crazy configurations, a customer who doesn't know how to double-click, etc...

The next step is to figure out, between the 5-10 hours per week you're spending on support, and the 40-50 hours per week you spend at work, how you're going to find time to add new features. The kicker is the support burden actually worsens with time because your customer base grows. After 1 month you have 100 customers with potential problems, after a year, 1,200.

And yes, the person you decided to sell to even though they complained about the high price ($25) is still hanging around, emailing you weekly wondering when the next release is coming.

But you persevere, and manage to slog your way through the incoming support requests and get started on new features.

What you find is that ongoing development, as with any legacy system, is much slower than green field development. You're now tied to legacy code and design decisions. You soon realize this isn't what you signed up for when you had that brilliant flash of insight that people need web-based software that helps them when locating their keys.

It's about this time that support emails start going unanswered, releases stop, and the product withers on the vine. It may wind up for sale on Flippa (www.flippa.com), or it may be relegated to the bone yard of failed software products.

The Upside

The flip side is what you've already heard on the blogs of successful product developers.

Once a product hits critical mass, you've conquered the hardest part of the equation. After that, the exponential leverage of software products kicks in and you can live it up on your empire of web-based unlocking-device locator applications. It's a recurring revenue stream that can grow far beyond what you would make as a consultant, all the while creating balance sheet value (meaning one day, you can sell it for stacks of proverbial cash and retire).

This is unlike your consultant buddy, whose consulting firm is worth 44 cents once she decides to retire because she had an unused stamp on her desk.

But there is a dip before you get to this place of exponential leverage and proverbial cash. A big dip. And if you can get through it once, it's more likely that you'll be able to get through it with your next product. And the one after that.

The key factor in getting you through the dip is your goals. These are the goals you wrote down six months prior due to the advice given to you in a random book about startups.

Once you make it to the other side, you've learned what it takes to launch and maintain a product. The next time you launch a product, you will have a monumentally better chance of success because you are now a more savvy software entrepreneur.

Why People Make the Switch from Developer to Entrepreneur

As a developer, your income, your ability to control what projects you work on, and your ability to control what you learn, end at a certain point.

For the first several years you're constantly learning, working on (seemingly) fun projects and your income grows quickly if you apply yourself.

But the experiences of many veteran developers show that after a certain level of experience you can't push past that financial barrier. And keeping up with the latest and greatest technology – something that used to excite you – will begin to wear you down.

It's hard to break out of that position and most often it requires a big risk. In my experience this risk involves joining an existing startup or starting one of your own.

I've tried both. I did it more for the excitement and freedom than for the income. In fact, I took a pay cut when I moved from consulting to owning my own products. But my passion for building something I own and the opportunity to experience true time and location independence far outweighed the drop in income.

Lack of Learning

Part of your "topping out" will likely be a lack of learning. While it's true there are always new technologies to learn, as you mature in your technology career it's likely you will begin to feel like a hamster on a wheel as you learn one more way to pull data out of a database. The idea of spending the time to learn how to do it using the latest method begins to make you tired.

It starts to feel as if you are constantly moving from one technology to the next which involves little "real" learning and a lot of learning some new syntax or API...things that will change in six month anyway. You start to feel like learning new techniques for the rest of your life will basically rehash the same things you learned in your first two years as a programmer.

Ownership

I like to use the analogy of renting vs. buying a home. When you rent you have less commitment, you can move often, and renting is typically less expensive than buying. But you don't own anything and you don't build equity. When you move out you're not any better off than when you moved in.

Such it is with salaried employment and consulting. When the day is done you own nothing. Not only does this translate into a lack of financial gain, it's a mental challenge as well. Many find it hard to build application after application and never feel passionate about the application they're building.

Once you launch a product, you are instantly building equity. With every copy you sell and every improvement you make, you are building something that will not only generate income in the future, but actually has value on the open market. Instead of having nothing at the end of your lease, you wind up getting back all of your rent money and more in equity.

The Biggest Roadblocks to Your Success

There are many roadblocks between the day you decide on a product idea and the day you launch. Your day job, family commitments, or the allure of the TiVo have a tendency to chip away at your grand ideas and leave you feeling overwhelmed, unproductive and unmotivated.

After 6 months of building your product with little more to show than a few thousand lines of plumbing code, it's easy to lose focus and shut the whole thing down.

The biggest roadblocks I've experienced first-hand or discovered through conversations with entrepreneurs are discussed below, along with strategies for how to avoid them.

Roadblock #1: No Market

This is by far the most common mistake I've seen – building something no one wants. We'll discuss the importance of having a market in more detail in chapter 2.

It's a common belief that building a good product is enough to succeed. It's not.

If you are the typical developer, you will not have enough money, power or fame to generate demand for a product people don't need or don't know they need.

How to Avoid It

Avoid this roadblock by building a product *after* you've verified there is a market.

In chapter 2 we'll look at the right questions to ask about a potential market, how to answer to those questions using research, and how to test the validity of your market for a minimal investment before you write your first line of code.

Roadblock #2: Fear

The first time you try something it's scary.

As humans we fear the unknown. We fear failure...rejection...mistakes. These are either feelings that come naturally or have been pressed into us by society.

This fear is what makes starting a company hard. It entails a large amount of risk with so much potential for failure, rejection and mistakes.

How to Avoid It

While there's no way to avoid the fear of starting your company, the following can help put the fear in perspective:

> *The up-front fear is a big indicator that you're going to grow as a person if you proceed through it. And, frankly, the terror wears off pretty quickly.*

It's true. Surprisingly, anything is much easier the second time. And the third. And by the fourth time you can't even feel the hair on the back of your neck, or the sweat in your palms because it's no longer there. The terror goes away surprisingly quickly.

The interesting thing is that the more you taste this growth, the more you want it. It's a rush, and it's addictive. .

It's a huge confidence boost to look back at the things that scared you last month, last year, or even five years ago. And realize you conquered them.

This kind of success leads you to trust your instincts. It builds confidence. It eliminates pointless analysis that used to keep you spinning on decisions for hours, days or weeks.

Overcoming the terror of firsts is hard, but it's what makes the goal beyond it worth achieving. The terror that stands between you and the goal is something 99.9% of people will never overcome.

Roadblock #3: Lack of Goals

Having no clear, written goals for your startup means you won't know whether to pursue the white label deal someone offers you two weeks after launch, or to start selling in overseas markets because someone asks you to.

Without goals for both yourself and your startup you are flying blind without guidance in situations where there is no right or wrong answer. Answers need to stem from your long-term desires for your startup and yourself.

- Want to grow as large as possible? Make that your goal and take advantage of every opportunity that comes your way. Realize this will mean hiring employees, and working longer hours.
- Want to spend more time with your family and quit your 9 to 5? Make that your goal and realize you will have to turn down many opportunities that come your way.

Your goals must serve as your roadmap that takes you to your definition of a successful startup.

How to Avoid It
You've already heard this a few times, but define your goals and *write them down*.

Roadblock #4: Inconsistency
The main problem with inconsistency is that it makes you lose momentum and momentum is critical to staying productive.

Forget the TV and video games. How many times have you found yourself thinking you were being productive only to look back and realize you spent 3 hours searching for and evaluating something you may not need until 6 months down the road?

Spending an evening finding 50 blogs to market to is a great way to feel productive, but do you really need 50, or could you get by with 10? Shouldn't you have outsourced this task for a pittance to any respectable virtual assistant (VA)? In reality, the 4 hours you spent researching should have been 10 minutes spent writing up this task.

The hard part is that it sure feels productive to spend 4 hours doing research and it's fun, to boot. Unfortunately, it doesn't get you closer to launching.

Another common distraction masquerading as productivity is reading business books. It sure seems like *Why We Buy*[6], *Made to Stick*[7] and *Outliers*[8] are going to help you launch a successful product. But reading books gets you no closer to launching than watching *Lost*.

If reading business books is a hobby, fantastic. But it won't get you one hour closer to launch.

How to Avoid It
You've likely heard of the concept of an information diet.

The idea is that most of the information we consume is a waste of time. Newspapers, magazines, blogs, podcasts, the news...are all enjoyable to consume, but they have a tendency to offer a constant distraction from real productivity.

You can't consume and produce at the same time – when you're in high-producing mode you have to temporarily step away from your magazines, blogs, and other forms of distraction for a while. Being in the pattern of checking your RSS reader every time you sit down at your computer kills hours of productivity each week. Those are hours that could be spent building your product.

It's not easy, but scaling back your information consumption will have a huge impact on your productivity.

Start by checking your RSS reader once a day and limit yourself to 30 minutes.

Limit your news reading and TV watching to X minutes (whatever you're comfortable with).

---

[6] http://tinyurl.com/23bxxtb

[7] http://tinyurl.com/2b8v2x2

[8] http://tinyurl.com/23w2oz7

Anytime you're on your computer ask yourself "Is this activity getting me closer to my launch date?"

Roadblock #5: Believing You Have to Do Everything Yourself

I'm in the process of buying a house. The house we made an offer on last week has 45 images I would like to share with family and friends, but they are hidden behind a questionable JavaScript interface. Using my advanced knowledge of web hackery (i.e. View Source), I grabbed the list of each image URL and put them in a text file. The following ten seconds made a huge difference in how I spent the next 20 minutes of my day.

I copied the first URL into my clipboard and began to paste it into my address bar when I (for the hundredth time) realized that this is exactly the kind of task that appears to produce something, but is completely rote and repetitive. It would be simple (and fun) to write a Perl script to do the fetching, but that would take around the same amount of time.

So I sent the task to my virtual assistant (VA). It took me exactly 90 seconds to get the request to him and within 24 hours, I had a zip file of the images. It took 20 billable minutes and at $6/hour the 24-hour wait was well worth it.

This morning I realized I needed an image for one of my websites and a change to the CSS. I'm not a great designer but I could have designed something in about two hours. I could have also made the CSS change and tested it in a few browsers in about an hour.

Instead, I opted to send these simple tasks to someone else at the cost of $15/hour. I wrote up an email and the task will be done in the next day or two.

- Time spent: 10 minutes
- Time saved: 2 hours, 50 minutes

How Much Can You Really Gain?

These are trivial examples of what I call *drip outsourcing*; outsourcing small tasks as I perform my daily work. Drip outsourcing has become invaluable to my productivity.

If you total up the three instances above it only amounts to 6-7 hours. But you can do this constantly, every day. Before I start any task I ask myself: "Could one of my contractors possibly do this?"

Over the course of a month you can easily save 20-40 hours without much effort. These days I save 60-100 hours a month.

The roadblock that so many entrepreneurs encounter as they try to launch is thinking *they, or one of their co-founders, has to perform every task necessary to get their product out the door.*

Just for kicks I'm going to spit out a list of tasks needed to take a web-based product from idea to your first week after launch. Here we go:

- Niche Brainstorming & Mental Evaluation
- Niche Evaluation
- Niche Selection
- Product Selection
- Product Architecture
- Functional Design
- Database Design
- Graphic Design*
- HTML/CSS*
- UI Development (AJAX/JS)*
- Business Tier Development*
- Database Development*
- Creating Unit Tests*
- Creating UI Tests*
- Manual Testing*
- Fixing Post-Launch Bugs*

- User Documentation
- Installation Documentation
- Sales Website Site Map Creation
- Sales Website Copywriting*
- Sales Website Graphic Design*
- Sales Website HTML/CSS*
- Sales Website Programming*
- Sales Website Payment Integration*
- Product Delivery (via email, link on site, etc...)*
- Setting Up Email List
- Setting Up Domain Name & Web Hosting
- Setting Up Email Accounts & 800 Number
- Setting Up Analytics
- Pre-Launch Search Engine Optimization
- Pre-Launch Pay-Per-Click Set-up
- Initial Social Media /Viral Marketing*
- Pre-Launch Video Marketing
- Pre-Launch Partnerships
- Launch Press Release*
- Pre-Launch Email Marketing
- Pre-Launch Blogging or Podcasting
- And probably a few others...

There is a list of 37 tasks ranging in duration from 2 hours to a few hundred.

You'll notice many of them have asterisks next to them. These are the tasks that will be easiest to outsource – the tasks that require a technical or common skill that's not specific to your product.

Outsource your product architecture? Only for small applications.

Outsource your graphic design and HTML/CSS? Every time...

How to Avoid It

The bottom line is to start small, gain comfort with a contractor, and gradually increase the amount you outsource.

Outsourcing is a learned skill, and you're likely to screw it up your first time around. Start with non-critical tasks and be very specific in how they should be executed. At first it will seem like you could do the tasks faster than the time it takes to assign them, but as you get to know the person you're outsourcing to it will quickly begin to save you time. If it doesn't, then you need to look for a new resource.

Hiring a Virtual Assistant (VA) is a great way to get started with almost no financial commitment and a low hourly rate (around $6/hour overseas, $10-20/hour in the U.S.). We'll discuss VAs more in chapter 6.

Graphic design and HTML/CSS are also great ways to dive in. Graphic design is nice because it's not complicated and what you see is what you get. It's either good or it's not. Design is much easier to outsource than programming.

Finding decent designers is a little more challenging than finding a VA – Elance[9] is a good route, but asking around is even better.

Take a risk this month: outsource your first task and see where it takes you. When was the last time a single tool or work habit offered the opportunity to save 20-60 hours?

Changing Your Time Mindset

It's a big leap moving from employee to entrepreneur. One of the biggest adjustments is accepting that time is your most precious commodity.

---

[9] www.elance.com

Dollarizing

The phrase "dollarize" is used in sales to describe the approach of showing your prospect how your price is less expensive than your competition due to the amount of money they will save in the long run.

For example, you can dollarize a screw[10] by showing how your deliveries are always on-time, your defect rate is half that of your competitors and your screws can withstand an additional 500 lbs. of stress, each resulting in time saved in material handling and warranty calls.

If you take it a step further and you possess the appropriate data, you can approximate how much money your screws will save your prospect in a given year based on the number of times your competitors deliver late and how many defects the customer will avoid by using your screws.

It's a powerful technique and a way to turn an otherwise commodity purchase into a bottom-line savings.

Dollarizing Your Time

In the same vein, dollarizing your time is the idea of putting a theoretical dollar amount on each hour you work. If you value your time at $100/hour it makes certain decisions, such as outsourcing work to a $6/hour virtual assistant, a no-brainer.

Putting a value on your time is a foundational step in becoming an entrepreneur, and it's one many entrepreneurs never take. Skipping this step can result in late nights performing menial tasks you should be outsourcing, and an effective hourly rate slightly above minimum wage.

It never seems like a good idea to pay someone out of your own pocket for something you can do yourself...until you realize the economics of doing so.

---

[10] Editor's Note: They do this extensively in Nevada.

Approaches to Dollarizing Your Time

There are two approaches to dollarizing your time. Choose the one that makes the most sense for your situation.

Approach #1: Freelance Rates

If you are a freelance developer or consultant, you probably have an hourly rate. This is a good place to start. If you bill clients $60/hour, then an hour of your time is worth $60.

If you don't perform freelance work, do a search on Craigslist or Guru[11] for freelancers *in your local area* with similar skills. As a developer with a few years of experience you'll likely see rates in the $40 and up range. Frankly, if you have no other information, $50/hour is a good number to start with.

Approach #2: Salary

If you don't perform freelance work or have difficulty finding comparative freelancers online, another approach is to divide your current salary + benefits by 2,000 (the approximate number of hours worked in a year), rounded up to the nearest $5 increment.

It varies widely, but a typical benefits package including 401k matching, disability insurance, health care, and time off can range from 20-45% of your salary. You can come close to determining the real dollar amount using your pay stub and a bit of math, but if you just want to take a swing at it use 30%.

So if your salary is $60,000 per year, 30% of that is an additional $18,000 making your effective salary $78,000. $78,000 divided by 2,000 gives you an hourly rate of approximately $39/hour, or $40/hour when rounded up to the nearest $5 increment.

Be aware that freelance rates are nearly always higher than salaried rates because freelancers spend a portion of their time

---

[11] www.guru.com

on non-billable tasks such as invoicing, marketing, sales, etc... They have to increase their billable rate to make up for these non-billable hours.

Ultimately it's up to you, but I would tend towards using the higher freelance rate for your time, especially since it's closer to what you would receive on the open market if you chose to pursue freelance work.

Keep in Mind: Desired Earnings

Realizing your time is worth $50/hour is the first step; the next step is actually generating $50 for every hour you work, and the third step is figuring out how to make your time worth $75 or $100/hour. If you continue to think your time is worth $50/hour it will to stay at $50/hour.

$100/hour is a good long-term goal to shoot for. If you've done your research on one-person software companies (which are similar in economics to small software startups), the reality for most tends to be closer to $25/hour[12].

If you are making $25/hour as an entrepreneur you are doing something wrong. Improve your marketing, grow your sales, find a new niche, outsource and automate. $25/hour is not an acceptable dollarized rate for a startup.

While you won't be earning anywhere near $50/hour when you begin building your product, once you launch you should aim to hit that number within 6 months. In the early stages, your dollarized rate is a mental state but you want to make it a reality as soon as possible. Once you've succeeded, then you can work towards increasing it.

Realizations

Several realizations stem from dollarizing your time.

---

[12] http://blog.businessofsoftware.org/2007/09/start-a-softwar.html

Realization #1: Outsourcing is a Bargain

Once you've established you're worth $50/hour, paying someone $6/hour to handle administrative tasks or $15/hour to write code seems like a trip to the dollar store.

Outsourcing aspects of your business is the single most powerful approach I've seen to increasing your true hourly rate as an entrepreneur. If I didn't outsource my administrative tasks, my effective hourly rate would plummet.

Realization #2: Keep Work and Play Separate

Wasting time is bad. Boring movies, bad TV, and pointless web surfing are expensive propositions. If you aren't enjoying something, stop doing it.

I need to re-iterate here: I'm not saying you should never relax, have fun, watch movies, play with your kids, watch TV, or surf the web. I'm saying that you should be deliberate about your work and your free time to get the maximum benefit from both. In other words:

> *Work hard and play hard, but never do both at once.*

Numerous times throughout the day ask yourself:

> *At this very moment am I making progress towards crossing off a to-do, -or- am I relaxing and re-energizing?*

If I'm doing neither, evaluate the situation and change it.

If you aren't enjoying a movie, walk out.

If you're playing with your kids and working on your iPhone you're not really working or playing – you're doing both poorly. Put the iPhone away and focus on your kids; it will shock you how much more fun you have and how, after making this choice, you'll feel energized and ready to dive back into work.

The same goes for multi-tasking work in front of the TV. Your productivity level is around 50% when trying to do both. Most evenings you'll feel as if you worked the whole night but didn't get anything done.

Realization #3: Wasting Time is Bad

If your time is worth, say $75/hour, standing in line at the bank is painful. Sitting in traffic is another money waster – every non-productive, non-leisure minute you spend is another $1.25 down the drain.

Since it's not practical to assume you will never wait in line again, the best counter-attack is to have a notebook and pen handy at all times. Use this time for high-level thinking, something you may have a hard time doing in front of a computer.

It's amazing that we think we can remember our important thoughts. Due to the amount of information and chaos you consume each day, a thought stays in your head for a few seconds before it disappears. Perhaps you will think of it again, perhaps not. Writing down important ideas is critical to building a list of ways to improve your business.

With a notebook in hand, you'll find yourself having amazing insights while in line at the post office.

For years I've carried a notebook everywhere I go for this exact purpose. I use it to capture keyword ideas, product ideas, niche ideas, to-do's, and any other valuable information that surfaces.

Again, I'm not saying you should be working all the time – if you want to bring a magazine to read in line, by all means do it. If your mind needs to rest when you're running errands then use this as a time to re-energize so you can hit your work harder when you return to it.

The real statement here is that you should never find yourself *killing time*.

Realization #4: Information Consumption is Only Good When it Produces Something

The following discussion excludes consumption for pleasure, such as: reading a novel, watching *The Daily Show*, catching a movie, etc.

Consuming and synthesizing are very different things; it's easy to consume in mass quantity. It's much more difficult to synthesize information.

Have you ever read through an entire magazine only to realize you can't remember any specifics about what you just read?

As someone who likely enjoys consuming in large quantities, at some point you will realize that you are wasting an enormous amount of time. I highly recommend putting the following into place:

> *When reading blogs or books or listening to podcasts or audio books, take action notes.*

Action notes are short- or long-term to-do items that apply directly to my businesses.

For example, I listen to several SEO podcasts. If they mention an interesting website, I make a note to check it out the next time I'm able.

As they mention a new SEO technique I create a specific to-do to try that approach on one of my websites. I make the action note specific so I can act on it quickly the next time I have a few spare minutes. If I were to write something general like "Google Webmaster Tools," it doesn't help me. But if I write "Create Google Webmaster Tools Account for DotNetInvoice," I can act on this quickly and cross it off my list without having to do much real thinking.

Action notes allow you to quickly determine which resources provide real value and which are fluff.

Since implementing action notes, I've canceled two magazine subscriptions, removed 40+ blogs from my RSS reader, and have become choosy about the audio books I buy.

This approach provides you with real-time feedback on the value of any consumable. A $4.99 audio book is actually a cost if it chews up 6 hours of your time and provides no actionable items.

Transitioning from Developer to Entrepreneur

You've likely realized that entrepreneurship and software development are two very different things. Software development is a subset of the skills an entrepreneur needs to launch and operate a successful startup.

If you've been writing code for years you've formed opinions and viewpoints that don't quite hold true in this new world. This lesson covers 9 realizations that will come to you at some point during your transition from developer to entrepreneur.

There's a lot of information here so don't feel as if you have to fully grasp everything today. If a few of them sink in and the rest prepare you for what's to come, you will be in a better position to succeed.

Realization #1: Being a Good Technician is Not Enough

In *The E-Myth Revisited*[13], author Michael Gerber talks about the archetypes of running a business. They are: entrepreneur, manager and technician.

- The **entrepreneur** is the dreamer, the visionary, and the creative mind.
- The **manager** is the person who thinks about return on investment (ROI), near-term success, and productivity.
- The **technician** gets the work done. She follows the manager's guidance and is concerned about today's success.

95% of us are comfortable, and probably excel at, being technicians. This means you're good at writing code, producing something tangible, and cranking away on each task, moving one step closer to launch date.

But it takes more than a technician to run a successful business. It's critical to look ahead into the near-term and determine which features or marketing efforts will provide the best ROI (manager), and to think out a year or more to determine the long-term direction of your business (entrepreneur).

The first step is to determine your goals and objectives as we've been discussing in this chapter.

Without planning, organizing, systematizing, outsourcing, and marketing, all things you will shy away from as a technician, you will never make it past the $25/hour pit that many startups fall into.

---

[13] http://tinyurl.com/2bzsda6

Realization #2: Market Comes First, Marketing Second, Aesthetic Third, and Functionality a Distant Fourth

The product with a sizeable market and low competition wins even with bad marketing, a bad aesthetic, and poor functionality. Think QuickBooks in the early days, or any niche product you've ever seen that looked like it was written by a six year old but sold thousands of copies.

In the same market, the product with better marketing wins. Every time.

In the same market with equal marketing, the product with the better design aesthetic wins. Sure, a few people will dig deep enough to find that the "ugly" product has better or more functionality, but the product that wins is the one that has the best looking website and user interface.

Functionality, code quality, and documentation are all a distant fourth. I know that this sounds sacrilegious to a software developer, but unless you're marketing to software developers, your order of importance is market, marketing, aesthetic, function.

Realization #3: Things Will Never Be As Clear As You Want Them to Be

Writing code is cut and dry. There are different ways to accomplish the same thing, but in general you know how you want your application to behave and you just need to get it there. Your constraints are constant – the compiler behaves the same way it did the last time you compiled.

By comparison entrepreneurship, especially the marketing side, is never this clear. As we'll discuss in chapter 2, marketing is about math and human behavior. The math part is straight-forward. It's the human behavior that's going to throw you for a loop.

Even the foremost marketing experts in the world are not sure whether people will buy a new product. People with 20, 30 and

40 years of experience still have to take their best guess at what will succeed. They have to try things out and adjust as they go. They often do small roll-outs to test audiences and adjust the product or the message before unleashing it on the world.

You will have to do the same and it will involve a lot of guesswork at the start. That's a hard pill to swallow when you're used to making decisions based on fact. Instead, you have to take your best guess; then measure and tweak.

And then do it 20 more times until you succeed.

Realization #4: You Can't Specify Everything...But You Do Need a Plan

As developers, most of us have experience with the waterfall method of building software – write a detailed spec and build it as specified. With waterfall development changes are painful and time consuming.

You may be using an agile methodology these days, which is more in line with entrepreneurship than the waterfall approach. Define a long-term goal (launch your product), look at the next set of tasks that will get you one step closer to that goal, work, and re-evaluate in a week.

Before launch you may be able to get by using the waterfall method, but post-launch it will be a disaster. This goes for your development, support, and marketing efforts. As an entrepreneur, your #1 advantage is reaction time, and the waterfall approach reacts too slowly.

You can't specify everything, but you do need a plan to get you to your next release.

Realization #5: You Need to Fail Fast and Recover

If you haven't already, you will soon need to accept you are going to fail a lot. You will make bad decisions, waste time, waste money, run ineffective ads, miss deadlines, and release buggy code. Each time this happens, you have to accept that you failed and move on.

The faster you fail and learn from your mistakes, the faster you will improve. Pretty soon your ads won't lose money, you'll get better at estimating level of effort, and you'll be sure to thoroughly test the complex parts of your code.

But you have to wade through that sea of failures before you can reach the other side. And this can be a hard thing to do.

Realization #6: You Will Never Be Done

Finishing a software product is a great feeling. The night you roll the new bits to the production server is indescribable. The feelings of relief, joy, and accomplishment are some of the most rewarding parts of developing software.

And you're never going to feel that way with your product.

Sure, you'll have releases and milestones. And you'll feel good the day you launch a new version.

But you will never feel "done." You will always have a list of features, marketing tests, potential partnerships, and new markets to take care of. And while the journey is itself a gift, never having the feeling of completion is something you need to get used to.

The idea of building an application and sitting back to collect a check is, unfortunately, a pipe dream. You have to continually invest in both your product and your marketing in order to remain successful.

Realization #7: Don't Expect Instant Gratification

The first month you launch you will be lucky to break $100 in revenue.

A product, marketing effort, and a reputation take time to build. But once they build they snowball such that the effort to launch a new version of your product is miniscule by comparison, and your chances of success are much higher.

Once you have 5 releases under your belt, 1500 targeted visitors every month, a 500 prospect mailing list, and hundreds of incoming links...surprise! Things are easier. Much easier.

The effort of getting a new product off the ground is exponentially more than launching a new product once you have resources and experience behind you.

Don't expect that your work is over the day after you launch. That's the day work really begins.

Realization #8: Process is King
Documenting repeatable processes for anything you will do more than once is essential to your sanity.

It's true; you *can* fly by the seat of your pants and get by, but it makes you a hostage to your work.

If you've ever been a manager you probably like process and understand its benefits. If you're a developer you probably dislike process or see it as a necessary evil.

Startups, being lean and mean, seem like the perfect place to eliminate documents, have no systems, and no processes...but that's far from the truth.

Without process it's impossible to delegate, difficult to bring on a business partner, and easy to make mistakes. With processes in place it's much easier to sell your product if/when you want to make an exit.

The fact is, creating processes will bring you freedom through the ability to easily automate and outsource tasks. We'll discuss this in chapter 6.

Realization #9: Nothing about a Startup is a One-Time Effort

Many of us have the dream of launching our startup, investing time in the marketing effort, and from that day forward being able to focus on writing code. The problem is, nearly everything about a startup requires ongoing effort.

You have to invest time every month into marketing, development, support, SEO, AdWords, and every other aspect of your business. The dream of building an app that never breaks, never needs new features and possesses auto-pilot marketing are possible, but they will not come by accident.

To get to the point of an automated startup you have to choose your niche and your product wisely, and invest a large amount of time outsourcing and automating your business. Even then, support and feature development is the easiest part to outsource; marketing is one of the most difficult.

Conclusion

Realizing the differences between development and entrepreneurship is something that will benefit you in the long run as you pursue your dream of starting a company.

Understanding and embracing the entrepreneurial mindset will go a long way toward preparing you for the chaos that is a startup.

Chapter 2

Why Niches Are the Name of the Game

Popularity vs. Success

If you listen to startup founders, you've heard for years about the importance of finding a market before building a software product.

I'm going to take it even further: the single most important factor to a product's success is not the founders, not the marketing effort, and certainly not the product.

It's whether there's a group of people willing to pay for it.

I mentioned in the previous chapter:

> *Market comes first, marketing second, aesthetic third, and functionality a distant fourth*

The sentence above describes something I call the *Market First Approach* and it underscores the importance of finding your market before you have any idea what you are building.

This is the opposite of the *Product First Approach* most developers take when trying to launch a startup; this is when you think of a great idea for an application that you spend nine months building, only to find that there's no one willing to buy it.

Market Comes First...

The product with a sizable market and low competition wins even with bad marketing, a bad aesthetic, and poor functionality. Think QuickBooks, Palm, or IE 5.5.

You can sell garbage to a hungry market and make money. However, it's not a sustainable strategy.

Luck is the Exception

But the statement "market comes first" doesn't take luck into account. Luck as in startups like Hot or Not[14], Plenty of Fish[15], Facebook apps where people throw sheep, and Twitter apps where people throw @shp.

These are "startups" where no one really understands why they became so popular; they just caught on. Like a pet rock or a hula hoop.

In these cases, the market doesn't matter because luck trumps everything. With luck on your side you don't need money, good marketing or a solid product. You just need to be lucky.

You either luck out that your idea goes viral (which happens to maybe 1 out of 10,000 startups) or that your idea is so brilliantly conceived and executed that people clamor to find their wallets because you've solved their problem so well.

Either way it's a complete crap shoot – you don't know your application is going to be wildly successful until it happens rather unexpectedly. The guy down the street with the same skill invests the same amount of time as you have and he has

[14] www.HotOrNot.com

[15] www.PlentyOfFish.com

1 million users after 3 months; you have 12, one of which is your mom.

Why would someone roll this million-sided die when there are approaches with a much higher success rate that provide nearly all of the same benefits?

Because high-growth startups are where the cool kids hang out. You dream of being the next startup poster boy or girl that gets mentioned on *TechCrunch.*

You won't wind up on the cover of *Fast Company* for writing a waste management application. But you can build a very lucrative income if people in the waste management industry need your application.

The Startup Lottery

With a "hot idea" startup the odds are overwhelmingly against ever getting funding, much less having a liquidity event that puts money in your pocket. Your reward for success needs to be enormous (enough to never have to work again) because your odds of success are 1 in 10,000 if not worse.

If you accept that and realize that the 80 hour weeks for a year (or three) at sub-market wages are worth the gamble, then do it. There is a ton of excitement and fun along the way, and a genuine passion and pride in building a startup like this...but it's a mathematically poor decision, not unlike buying a lottery ticket. The odds are very much against you, worse than any bet you can place at the race track.

But there are still those who go for the VC-funded "hot idea" startup. Aside from the cool factor why might we pursue it?

I know a handful of people – including myself – who have reached for the VC-backed startup life. Each of us did it for one, *maybe* two startups (you can only do so many before you burn out). Not surprisingly, none of us "made it."

Based on conversations with these friends, the reasons given for pursuing this path are the same ones I gave back when I started pursuing this road with a couple Yale MBAs. They fall into two categories:

1. The "lottery" factor of hitting it big and cashing out
2. Popularity; having everyone talk about you

The first reason implies that you're going to do something with the money you make. My guess is you would either plan to stop working and retire to Tahiti, or continue working only on projects you enjoy. So why not work on a project you enjoy right now?

The second reason is popularity. This one is up to you. If you want popularity enough to diminish your chance at success then that's your choice. But we won't be covering that path in this book.

There are many ways to get to success that don't involve VC funding: becoming a Micropreneur or bootstrapper are the two ways we'll look at in this book.

Even folks you've likely never heard of like Stephane Grenier[16] or David Michael[17] make a good living with real software products that fill a market's need. They're not going to sell out for $10 million, but they're doing all right financially and have all the benefits you'd expect from owning a business: passion, flexibility, freedom, and so on.

The common thread to all of the entrepreneurs I've named so far is *that they have found a group of people willing to pay for your software.*

---

[16] www.followsteph.com

[17] www.davidrm.com

Back to Basics

Fast Company would have you believe that the "million users in 3 month" scenario is the best way to build a startup (because it makes a good story and sells magazines).

But the way the vast majority (dare I say 99.5%) of all businesses in this world that succeed in the long-term – be they large or small, high-growth startup or lifestyle business – is to find a market that is willing to pay them money for *something*.

That *something* can be dry cleaning services, invoicing software, or hosted salesforce automation. What matters is finding a group of people who need your *something* more than they need the money you're charging for it.

How do you find those people? We'll discuss that below.

But once you find them, provide your product with no hassles at a price where you make a healthy profit and you're set.

Niches Are the Name of the Game

You've probably had a great idea similar to the following (an almost true-to-life transcript of my thoughts four years ago):

> *"The world needs an online accounting application. I'm going to build QuickBooks for the web.*
>
> *Let's see...I know I can code a killer AJAX interface, the DB tables will be simple...I've built apps like this before. 1.0 shouldn't take more than a couple months."*

Luckily, before I wrote a line of code I ran copious Google searches. Sure enough, even four years ago there was serious competition in this space. There are some big players with healthy development staffs, sizable venture capital bankrolls, and a heck of an edge given their thousands of paying customers.

Building a general purpose, small-business, online accounting application is a really bad idea for a self-funded startup. For one, you won't have the development or marketing resources to compete with the likes of Freshbooks, Blinksale, and BillMyClients. In addition, you won't be able to keep up with support or feature implementation for that many general purpose business clients.

Enter Niches

A better approach would be to pick a niche market like web designers and build an online accounting system that in every way caters to them. Make the site user friendly, the graphics unbelievable, and have a bunch of pre-set invoice items that relate to designers.

Or how about catering to therapists? Therapists have complex billing situations and often deal with insurance companies; surely you could build an online solution better than the 12-year old desktop software available to them today (note: this is a real business idea I've had for about three years – I think there's potential to make a killing).

With either of these strategies you'd be selling to a smaller market but you'd be able to charge more for your product. Word of mouth would be a huge factor, and you will likely know precisely where to find your market in high concentration (you can probably list 5 sites off the top of your head where web designers hang out).

And you can make this niche market really, really happy.

If you choose a niche market and focus so tightly that your product becomes the best in class, members of that niche will have no choice but to use your product.

Reasons You Must Go Niche

The following are the main reasons Micropreneurs and bootstrappers should stick to niches and run screaming for the hills from large markets.

Reason #1: A Niche Requires You to Narrow Your Product Focus

Here's an exercise: Pick one person you know well...your spouse, your brother, your sister, a parent, etc.

How hard would it be to design a product that you're *sure* this person would use...not very hard, right? That's because you know so much about the intimate details of their life.

Based on your knowledge of their interest in playing death metal on the banjo, for example, you might build a website that aggregates every death metal banjo tablature on the web (tablature is like sheet music).

Or you might build software that displays common death metal banjo chords.

Either way, you'd have a really good shot at making something that they can't live without simply because of your intimate knowledge of their interests. And odds are, since your product would be so laser focused to their interests, it wouldn't already exist.

Think about it another way; which of the following are *you* more likely to buy?

1. A book about marketing
2. A book about marketing products
3. A book about marketing software
4. A book about marketing niche software products written by a small startup team and sold mostly over the internet

Judging by the fact you're reading this, I would guess #4.

The lesson here is that the narrower you can make your product while still maintaining a large enough market, the more profit you will generate. It's that simple – if you can find a small group of people and make them amazingly happy, *you will make money.*

Would you rather sell your software to 100% of the people in a 5,000 person niche, or 10% of the people in a 50,000 person niche?

The correct answer: 100% of the people in a 5,000 person niche.

The reason? It's cheaper to advertise to 5,000 people, and the odds are higher that they all hang out in the same place, be it a website, forum, blog, or magazine. The competition is also a lot lower.

Reason #2: Niche Advertising is more Cost Effective
The most common mistake made by inexperienced marketers is attacking a market that's too large. Common sense tells you that the larger your market is, the better off you are. For bootstrapped startups, the opposite is true.

Marketing to large markets is not cost-effective. The larger a market, the more money you'll need to spend in order to locate people willing to buy your product.

Let's say you've built an iPhone application for people who like to travel. It has figures, maps, guides, and currency calculators...everything you need to get around a new place. Since you're marketing to every traveler in the English-speaking world, you might want to take out an ad in *Travel + Leisure Magazine*. If so, be prepared to drop $106,000 for a full-page ad.

And odds are that most people who see your ad won't be interested.

Add the fact that you'll be competing against huge companies like Princess Cruises and Travelocity – companies with entire teams dedicated to making their ad look way better than yours – and it's obvious that it's not a good investment.

Note: I don't recommend magazine ads for startups; this is simply an example to show the value of narrowing market focus

Instead of marketing to everyone who likes to travel, how about tailoring your product to people who like to travel to the American Northwest?

A one-page ad in Northwest Magazine runs $2,897. The fact that it's 36x cheaper not only puts it in the realm of possibility for you, but eliminates large competitors and implies your market is smaller and more focused.

> *Odds are high that if a publisher started a magazine aimed at a niche, and full-page ads are less than $5,000, it's a good niche to explore.*

Advertising to this smaller audience is going to garner more "actions per view." If you provide something so uniquely targeted towards them you can focus the ad itself, your copy, and your product on what they need, they are more likely to visit your website.

Looking at it from the Pay-per-click (PPC) angle, bidding on "travel" in Google AdWords will yield around 3 million ad views per month at a cost of around $1.75 per click. Suffice to say, you probably don't have the $146,000 – $239,000 Google estimates to rank in the top 3 ads for this term.

But how about the approximately 5,000 people who searched for a variation of "Oregon travel" on Google last month? At around $1.25 per click, and $110-180 to cover the keyword for the month...it's probably more in-line with your budget and people who click on your ads are highly targeted buyers.

Reason #3: Niches Have Less Competition

The market for word processors is pretty much sewn up, wouldn't you say? Microsoft put the nail in the coffin of Lotus Notes and WordPerfect years ago.

So how do we explain Nota Bene[18], a thriving word processor with a hideous website that sells for $399? (compare to the $79 you'll pay for Microsoft Office Home 2007, which includes 3 other applications)

Nota Bene is a niche word processor for academics and researchers with advanced support for bibliographies and citations. *Microsoft* wouldn't touch a niche this small with a 10-foot pole; they aren't set up to be profitable in tiny markets like this.

If a market is less than $100 million or so you won't find Microsoft. This, and much smaller markets, are the spaces where your startup will thrive.

Owning the majority of a $500,000/year market is enough to support a very profitable startup, especially one that's taken no outside funding.

Reason #4: Niches Have Higher Profit Margins

In the example I gave above with Nota Bene, did you notice that *Nota Bene* costs a lot more than Microsoft Word? ($399 for Nota vs. $79 for Office Home).

Nota Bene is not as easy to use, nor as pretty, nor as powerful as Word. So how can it be priced so much higher? Because Nota Bene is one of the only players in the academic word processing niche.

---

[18] www.NotaBene.com

It's not that Dragonfly Software (the makers of Nota Bene) is gouging their customers; they are a small software company and as a result their cost per copy sold is much higher. At the same time, they are able to push the limits of their pricing since their audience, knowing they are looking for a niche product, is willing to pay more than they would ever consider paying for a general word processing tool.

In addition, the laser-focused utility of Nota Bene, the fact that it solves a very specific and painful problem for its customer base, makes it well worth the $399 (if you've ever tried to manage a bibliography in Word you'll know what I mean).

In general, since niche markets are small they have less competition, and less competition means you are able to charge more for your product, resulting in higher margins.

Reason #5: Niche Markets Are Not Used to Good Marketing
Have you ever compared the ads in the *New York Times* to the ads in your local paper?

How about the national ads run during the *Super Bowl* vs. the ads your local car dealer runs during the 6 O'clock news?

Niche markets are typically pursued by small players; players who don't have the marketing expertise (or the manpower) of large companies. As a result, competing in niche markets is a lot easier than running head-to-head against someone like Monster.com (whose well-produced commercials run each year during the *Super Bowl*).

Reason #6: It's Easier for Prospects to Trust You
In smaller markets it's easier to make a name for yourself since people are more likely to hear about you multiple times in a shorter time period.

If you take out an ad on websites they visit, advertise on *AdWords* for similar keywords, and have a *Facebook* group, in a small niche it's likely they'll run into you more than once over a short period of time.

There's an old marketing theory that says prospects need to hear your message seven times before they remember you, but in this day and age I think it's different.

These days, when I hear about a movie from a friend, I tend to disregard it. The second time I hear about it I'm intrigued, especially if it's on a topic of interest to me. The third time, before they can finish, I've logged on and added it to my Netflix queue.

Given the number of marketing messages we hear every day, hearing about anything more than once has become remarkable.

Exercise
A "warm" niche is a niche where you have some kind of association. Perhaps you worked for a credit card company for a few years, your wife is a lawyer, you collect comic books, or your brother is a plumber.

Each of these would be considered a warm niche, and introducing a product into this niche will be much easier than choosing a completely unknown market. Remember, you stand a better chance when you know who you're selling to.

Make two columns on a piece of paper. In the header of the left column write "Person" and in the right one write "Hobby or Work Experience."

Now for each row write the name of someone you know, including yourself, friends, relatives or colleagues, and write their work experience or hobby in the right column.

These are your warm niches. You'll need them later in this chapter.

A Look at Finding Niche and Product Ideas

The most popular question I receive from early stage entrepreneurs is: how do I find a niche? I often hear the sentiment that all the good niches have been taken.

The challenge is that when you're starting out you want a crystal clear indication that the niche you choose is going to work. You're putting a lot of your time on the table and you want to make sure your niche is viable. You want a formula that takes in a few inputs and determines exactly the right niche for you.

Although I can tell you the steps to follow to explore different niches, finding a niche and deciding on a product is all about marketing, and marketing is a fuzzy, imprecise discipline.

There is a leap of faith you'll have to take during the process of product selection where there's not going to be a perfectly laid road paved in gold. At some point you have to make your best guess and go with your gut feeling based on the data you've put together.

As I said in the last chapter: *things will never be as clear as you want them to be.*

Brainstorming Niches

A few paragraphs ago we looked at the process of coming up with warm niches. This is a critical piece – without a niche "insider" your chances of success are dubious at best. But that doesn't mean you can't entertain niches that may not be warm. You can always work your network to make a cold niche into a warm one.

Coming up with your initial list of niches amounts to pulling ideas out of thin air. Here are a few suggestions on how to do that.

Approach #1: Look at All Areas of Your Life

Examine your hobbies, interests and work experience. Are you into sports, the news, comic books, arts and crafts, health or shopping? Are you fascinated by modern art? Do you have experience building software for dentists?

Any of these can be a place to start.

Pamela Slim, of the *Escape from Cubicle Nation* blog[19] and podcast[20], has a six-minute look at choosing a business idea[21] that I highly recommend. Her process takes some time over the course of a month, but it's worth the effort to gather information about your interests.

Approach #2: Look at Occupations

Scan through the following lists of occupations to determine if you have any experience with them, or if you know someone who does:

- http://en.wikipedia.org/wiki/List_of_occupations
- http://www.bls.gov/news.release/ocwage.t01.htm

Approach #3: Cheat

One way to avoid the multi-step process of brainstorming niches, evaluating demand and selecting a product is to jump right to a product idea. And why not start with some inspiration to stretch and mold into a niche you're familiar with?

- http://www.entrepreneur.com/businessideas/ – Business idea search engine. I found the best ideas searching on Category->Online Businesses.

---

[19] www.escapefromcubiclenation.com

[20] escapefromcubiclenation.libsyn.com

[21] tinyurl.com/2cu2dn6

- http://www.sixmonthmba.com/2009/02/999ideas.html – A list of 999 product ideas. Only a portion are software/website ideas, but even the physical product ideas get your mind thinking about specific niches.
- http://www.ahbbo.com/ideas.html – Over 400 home business ideas. More of a generator of niche ideas than product ideas.
- http://ycombinator.com/ideas.html – Startup ideas YCombinator would like to fund.

For ongoing inspiration, I subscribe to every one of the following blogs. Even when I'm not prepared to build a product I scribble a note about an idea that I keep for review when I'm ready to build my next application.

- http://astartupaday.wordpress.com/ (also on Twitter at http://ww.twitter.com/astartupaday) – by far my favorite web app idea blog. I've come very close to pursuing several of his ideas exactly as he's written them.
- http://ideas.4brad.com/ – crazy ideas from Brad Templeton
- http://www.ideaisqueen.com/wordpress/ – I've seen quite a few ideas that would work for a Micropreneur on this blog.
- http://www.ideatagging.com/ – Another solid idea blog.
- http://springwise.com/ – Covers innovations in products and business models. Think about applying the innovations they mention to a niche from your list.
- http://www.trendwatching.com/ – A high-level look at emerging consumer trends.
- http://www.coolbusinessideas.com/ – Another list of business ideas that are already being implemented by someone.

Making it Easier to Find a Niche

The Best Niches are Reserved for People Who Do Something

My blog gets over 60 visitors per month who arrive based on a variation of the term "make your own magazine cover" based on a 36 word post I published four years ago.

I would never have guessed this is such a popular topic. And my blog has only hit on this single keyword phrase for it – imagine if you launched a strategic attack on every keyword combination you could think of surrounding the creation of magazine covers?

Maybe you would sell a downloadable app, or maybe a website where people would pay by the cover. Outsource some high end cover templates to a designer, and allow someone to create a cover for free, but pay $.99 to export to PDF, $4.99 to have a glossy copy mailed to their home (or the home of a friend), and $9.99 for an annual pass to save as many covers to PDF as they want. You could even charge $19.99 for a T-shirt of the cover.

You might add a social component and allow people to compete against one another and vote on the most popular covers. Invite designers to design their own covers...there is a lot of potential here if you let your mind loose.

I would never in a million years think of this niche, except for 36 words I wrote in late 2005.

Everyone is using the same keyword tools so good niches are found and taken pretty quickly. The best niches are *under the radar*, and you have to get out and do *something* before you will find them.

Evaluating a Niche

Given that you'll be focusing on a niche markct, the next step is to consider the cost of marketing to a specific niche. In this lesson you'll learn how to determine if a market is viable by deciding whether you can use the most cost-effective tools to market to it.

The Blue Chip Approach

If you worked in the product marketing department of Proctor & Gamble, one of the largest consumer product manufacturers in the world, you would be well acquainted with focus groups, eight-figure advertising budgets, and nine-figure target markets (hundreds of millions).

In this scenario, where TV and radio ads, billboards, and naming a sports arena after your company are advertising options, the goal is not to find a group of people looking for your product, but to create demand for your product by marketing to...well...pretty much everyone.

This approach, while not only expensive, has lost much of its effectiveness in recent years as consumers have become more and more immune to interruption marketing (that is, marketing that tries to interrupt someone during their daily life rather than speak to them at the exact moment when they are searching for a solution to a problem).

The Micropreneur Methodology

Even though this approach is called the *Micropreneur Methodology*, it applies equally to Micropreneurs and bootstrappers.

In the case of a self-funded startup you don't have the luxury of enormous ad budgets so you need tools that help you to determine in advance if people are looking for a solution to a

> *As a self-funded startup you want a market that is already looking for your product, even if it doesn't exist.*

particular problem. Do you notice the difference here?

This is because creating demand is very, very expensive while filling existing demand is, by comparison, cheap.

The other problem with TV, radio, magazine, and billboard ads is that they are hard to measure. If you pay $20,000 for a billboard, and the campaign is running simultaneously with 5 other marketing efforts, how can you tell which one is driving visitors to your website, or which one is driving paying customers?

There's another layer here – it's not just that offline marketing (marketing through avenues other than the internet) is expensive; it's also difficult to tweak, improve, and make a profit with as a small business.

So the question becomes: how can you read a market's mind? How can you peer into the thoughts of millions of people and determine if there is a demand for your product idea?

The answer, of course, is the internet – the largest collection of market information on the planet. Let there be no mistake: without the internet, everything we talk about in this book is

> *If your target market is not online, you have no chance of succeeding using the methodologies you'll find in this book.*

impossible. In fact, let me go so far as to say:

This is non-negotiable. Any target market you choose must be online and you must have a product that solves their problem.

Narrowing Further
Given the complexity of selling to large companies and government agencies you're going to want to narrow your focus to consumers, small businesses, or in certain cases, both.

These demographics have purchasing authority, make fast purchasing decisions, and search for solutions online. From a startup's perspective they are fantastic demographics.

With this in mind, there are two questions you need to answer about a potential niche:

- Is the market large enough?
- Is there an inexpensive way to reach them?

Is the Market Large Enough?

When searching for a niche, there's a loose rule of thumb that says to stick to markets where you can take out a full-page ad in a magazine targeted at your market for less than $5,000.

The idea is that if a market has a magazine devoted to it, it's large enough to provide enough customers and if a full-page ad is less than $5,000, the market is small enough that you'll be able to effectively market to it.

As an aside, I don't recommend magazine advertising due to the difficulty of tracking prospects, the inability to tweak content mid-stream, and the challenge of getting people to "switch media" from print to the web. But understanding how magazine publishers segment the market will provide you with insight into viable niches.

Magazine publishers are *in the business* of market segmentation. You didn't think the $10/year you pay for *Fast Company* comes close to paying their printing and shipping costs, right? No, they're in the business of reaching the maximum number of demographically "similar" people so they can increase ad rates.

As a result, if you're targeting a niche that has a magazine devoted to them, such as bass fishermen or ASP.NET programmers, you're on the right track.

The inverse of this rule does not hold true. In other words, if a niche does not have a magazine devoted to it, it's not necessarily too small. But a magazine offers a great starting point for getting inside your customers' thought process and also comes with the bonus of typically having a website where you can advertise.

Beyond searching for a magazine that caters to your market, you should also look at census and labor statistics to get an estimate of your market size. It's important to remember during this process that a large market is not helpful if you can't reach them economically through a specific website or magazine.

Your "market size" research should involve the following:

- A web search for related magazines and websites
- Tracking down their advertising rate cards, which tell you how much it will cost to advertise in their magazine or on their website
- Reviewing their circulation (for magazines), visitor statistics (for websites), and rates
- Entering websites without rate cards into Compete.com[22] to check traffic levels
- Checking in with your friendly neighborhood bureau of labor statistics for a sanity check on your findings

For example, if you were targeting marriage and family therapists in the U.S. you would spend a few hours on Google searching for "family therapist magazine" and "marriage therapist magazine." You would visit their websites and compile their rate cards. Rate cards are almost always available from a magazine's website. Look in the footer for a link to "rate card," "advertising" or "ad rates." The rate card

---

[22] compete.com

typically comes as a PDF and contains a lot of demographic information about the magazine's subscriber base.

If it's not available on their website (which I've only seen with small publications), email directly and ask for their rate card and circulation information (including web stats).

There is a huge book that comes out every year with this information but it's quite expensive ($1900) and is a bit out of date after 6-9 months. If you're taking a trip to your local library you can check it out in the reference section under the title *The Standard Periodicals Directory*.

Next, you should visit the U.S. Bureau of Labor Statistics[23] and search for Occupational Employment Statistics. A couple clicks later and you find there are 23,240 Marriage and family therapists in the U.S (as of April, 2009).

This may sound like a small number (out of 300 million people), but it can be deceiving as there are other classifications such as *Substance abuse and behavioral disorder counselors* and *Mental health counselors* that fit this market, depending on the nature of your product.

Given the number of publications and websites aimed at therapists and the Labor data, they are an excellent niche market. In fact, targeting a niche within this niche (such as young therapists who are starting their first practice) may even be an option here. From my research, a Web-2.0 therapist billing application has serious potential.

Be wary of a market if you are unable to find a handful of websites or a magazine/journal dedicated to it, and the labor statistics claim less than 10,000 members.

---

[23] www.bls.gov

To conclude, here are the best online resources for researching employment and demographic data:

- **U.S. Bureau of Labor Statistics** (www.bls.gov)
- **FreeLunch.com** (http://www.economy.com/freelunch/default.asp) - U.S. Only Economic and Financial Data
- **International Labour Services Library Services** (http://www.ilo.org/dyn/lfsurvey/lfsurvey.home) – Labor stats from around the globe
- **LABORSTA Internet** (http://laborsta.ilo.org/) – More labor stats from around the globe
- **U.S. and International Statistics Agencies** (http://www.bls.gov/bls/other.htm#International) – Labor and other statistics from around the globe

Is There an Inexpensive Way to Reach Them?

The second question you need to ask about a potential market is: how will you reach them in an inexpensive, sustainable manner?

When I talk to people who are thinking about launching a startup, from time to time I hear that if they could get to the front page of Digg[24] or get a mention on TechCrunch[25] they would be "set."

The problem is, your market is most likely not the people who read Digg. Nor the people who read TechCrunch.

When I've been on the front page of Digg, more than 90% of that traffic has stayed on my site for *less than 5 seconds*. That's not a market, that's a drive by.

---

[24] digg.com

[25] techcrunch.com

When you receive 50,000 visitors from one of the major media sites you will be lucky to convert five sales. Five measly sales. That has to win for the worst conversion rate ever.

The reason? *They are not your market.*

When looking at your marketing plan you should actually be thinking:

> *"If I could get only on the front page of [small-but-very-focused-niche-website].com."*

Find the website(s) where your *real* market hangs out. These are the people who will actually buy your product. The competition will be less and your conversion rates will be orders of magnitude higher.

Unfortunately, great products are often built and launched without a thought given to how the target audience will find out about it. You must have an inexpensive, ongoing source of new customers.

There are hundreds of ways to market software, but for Micropreneurs and bootstrappers there are a handful of what I call *Top Shelf* approaches, that we'll look at closely in this book. These approaches are the best way to provide sustainable, long-term prospects to your business.

The *Top Shelf* approaches focus on two key areas: building an audience and search engine optimization.

The good news about these approaches is that while they will bring in sustainable traffic, there are also shortcuts that will allow you to easily test a startup idea for a small investment (typically around $100).

Other marketing approaches abound, which I call *Second Shelf* approaches. They include:

- Building internet buzz and referral traffic
- Joint venture partnerships
- Article marketing
- Cold calling
- And so on...

These approaches will generate additional revenue for you, but without one of the Top Shelf approaches, you will have a difficult time generating a sustainable stream of prospects.

So the answer to whether or not there is an inexpensive way to reach your market is another question: can they be reached by building an audience such as a mailing list, blog, podcast or video blog, or through search engine optimization?

We'll look at how to answer this question later in this chapter.

Why Vertical Markets are better than Horizontals

If you're not familiar with the terms *vertical market* and *horizontal market*, fear not; they are marketing jargon that we'll clear up in this section.

- Think of a *vertical market* as a single industry or hobby. Examples of vertical markets include pool cleaners, dry cleaners, web designers, wine collectors and punk rock enthusiasts.
- By contrast, a *horizontal market* cuts across many industries or hobbies. General purpose invoicing software is a horizontal market since it can be used by pool cleaners, dry cleaners, and web designers.

From a startup perspective, vertical market niches are superior to horizontal markets for a number of reasons we'll look at below.

Reason #1: Members of a Vertical Have Similar Behavior

Since pool cleaners tend to come from similar backgrounds or follow a similar career path, they will tend to exhibit similar behavior when faced with a purchase decision. This also means that a single marketing message will more easily catch their attention than if you are trying to market software to both pool cleaners and web designers.

This is not to imply that all pool cleaners react and behave identically, but when compared to web designers they have many more similarities in how they view the world, how much web and technical expertise they possess, and how they decide on purchase decisions.

This ultimately means your marketing and sales approach can be simpler than if you are trying to cut across verticals.

Reason #2: Members of a Vertical Talk to One Another

Small industries tend to have a handful of thought leaders. Even industries like pool cleaners or countertop installers have business owners who are pushing the industry forward, finding and adopting new techniques, and communicating those techniques to the rest of the industry through conferences, trade shows, trade publications, online forums, social networks or mailing lists.

This is important for a business selling into this industry for two reasons:

1. If your product is good, word of mouth marketing will spread quickly
2. If you can find the thought leaders and convince them to adopt your product, you will receive massive exposure in a short period of time

Reason #3: Members of a Vertical "Hang out" Together

Pool cleaners hang out together; whether at local trade meetings, national conferences, or online. Having a handful of places where they congregate makes marketing much easier since you can simply attend (or sponsor) trade meetings or conferences.

Alternatively, you can also hang-out (or buy ads) in any online venues where a concentration of your target market aggregates.

This is an entrepreneur's dream.

The other benefit is that if you decide to use direct mail, cold calling or direct email marketing, there are lists available for specific industries. These lists will likely convert well if your product is targeted at the niche. Contrast this with owning a general small business invoicing solution – how do you buy a list for every small business in the U.S. without going broke?

It's much easier to target a specific industry (such as pool cleaners); your marketing expenses will be a fraction of the cost and will convert at a much higher rate.

Reason #4: Members of a Vertical Have Similar Needs
Imagine building an invoicing application for every small business in the world. The number of features would be overwhelming. How can you possibly provide a solution that works for pool cleaners, web designers and dry cleaners at the same time?

By contrast, building an invoicing solution that satisfies every single pain point for pool cleaners is not that difficult. They have well-defined needs that are common to pretty much anyone who services pools for a living. Building an application that satisfies their needs exceptionally well is a feasible task for a one or two person development team.

Are Horizontal Markets Ever a Good Choice?
This is not to say that you should *never* choose a horizontal market. But if you are considering this approach I would advise you to take another look at your warm niches and try to restrict your product to a vertical. As a general rule, horizontal

markets are too large and expensive for self-funded startups to navigate.

Measuring Market Demand Without Spending a Dime

Before We Begin

There is more information on niche research than you could consume in a lifetime. Every SEO book, blog, and website has their take. Every expert has a product or service that can help you with niche research. The importance of finding and marketing to a niche using search engine keywords (which we'll look at below) is well known and critical to millions of people trying to market online.

My guess is that you're not interested in a 300-page, all-encompassing treatise on keyword research. The reason I'm here is to distill information into an easily consumable form, a succinct list of *best tools and practices* for doing this research, rather than attempting to provide an extensive reference on the subject.

With niche research the problem is not finding new ideas, but narrowing to the most effective strategies that you can implement in a reasonable amount of time. That's what I've done with the technique below.

> *Given that we're in the process of narrowing our choices by exploring multiple niches with minimal time investment and no cash outlay, we are looking for a quick, easy and free way to determine a rough order of magnitude traffic and revenue estimates.*
>
> *This is what the Micropreneur Methodology provides.*

During the course of this discussion we will cover several disparate topics that are related by the umbrella of *Measuring Demand*. Below are the high-level topics we'll be discussing as we follow this path:

- **Conversion Rates** - The ratio of people who buy vs. visit your website
- **Traffic Levels** - A look at the level of traffic you might need to succeed in a particular niche
- **Traffic Breakdown** – A look at common percentages that different traffic sources might provide to your site

Everything You Need to Know About Sales
You only need to master two skills to sell online: human behavior and math.

Understanding **human behavior** means you know how people think, what motivates them. You need to know how to speak to the voice inside of them that makes buying decisions, rather than their tough, rational exterior. We will cover this in chapter 4 when we look at building a sales website.

Math is the science behind every business in the world, whether they realize it or not. With internet marketing, the math involves views, clicks, click through rates, unique visitors, goals, conversion rates, gross profit and net profit.

In this chapter…*it's all about Math.*

In this book we will not only evaluate demand for a niche without spending a dime, we will also learn the math behind determining if a niche is viable. And to understand that we have to start at the beginning.

Conversion Rates
The term "conversion rate" technically refers to the ratio of the number of people who visit your website to the number that perform a specific task. That task can be anything you

choose…signing up for your mailing list, trying your online demo, buying your product, etc…

For the purposes of this book, unless otherwise specified, *conversion rate* will refer to the percentage of website visitors who buy your product.

We're starting with conversion rate because it gives you an idea of the kind of traffic you need to build a viable business.

For example, if you sell a $10 product and have a 5% conversion rate, you need 1,000 visitors per month to make $500:

1,000 visitors x .05 x $10 = $500

Conversion rates vary based on a number of factors including the source of the traffic, your sales website's effectiveness, and whether your product is properly priced. But to give us a starting point, here are some general guidelines:

If your price point is in what I refer to as *the consumer range* of $1 to $50 and your product is priced appropriately for your market, your conversion rate should be between 1% and 4%.

If you're priced between $50 and $1,000 or offer recurring pricing and your product is priced appropriately for your market, you'll most likely convert between 0.5% and 2%.

These numbers vary, and will be skewed downward if your URL hits the front page of *Digg*, or skewed upward if you send a targeted mailing.

Some Actual Conversion Rates
Here are examples of actual conversion rates from a few sites I've been involved with:

- **FeedShot**[26] is a blog directory submission service I launched in 2005 and sold in 2007. It has a conversion rate of just below 3% on a price point of $2.
- **Just Beach Towels**[27] is an e-commerce website I owned. It had a conversion rate of around 2.5% with an average order size of about $20.
- **DotNetInvoice**[28] is my $329 invoicing software package. It converts between 0.5 and 0.7%.

Traffic

To give us a concrete example, let's take a downloadable product with a price point of $200.

The question is: how many visitors do you need to gross $1,000?

Let's assume your initial conversion rate is 0.5% due to your high price point. In that case you need 1,000 visitors to gross $1,000, as follows:

$$1,000 \text{ visitors} \times .005 \times \$200 = \$1,000$$

There is more going on here that we'll address right now. If your product is priced poorly for your target market your conversion rate will be lower than 0.5%. We will discuss pricing in a later lesson, but for now let's assume that $200 is a good price point for your product.

While we can't say for sure what your conversion rate will be at a specific price point, we can take an educated guess and obtain a ballpark number of visitors you need to shoot for to build a viable business.

---

[26] www.feedshot.com

[27] www.justbeachtowels.com

[28] www.dotnetinvoice.com

The thing to think about here is that we're not looking for exact numbers. Marketing is not programming; there are no exact numbers when projecting conversions.

Remember that we're in the process of narrowing our choices by exploring multiple niches with a minimal time investment and no cash outlay. We are looking for a quick, easy and free way to determine the approximate magnitude of traffic and revenue estimates. To achieve this, we get to use a bit of science and bit of educated guesswork.

Traffic Breakdown
You can divide website traffic into four categories:

- **Search Engines** – Organic searches on Google, Yahoo!, etc...
- **Incoming Links** – Organic links from blogs, directories, or any other website.
- **Direct Traffic** – Someone types your URL into the address bar of their browser.
- **Advertising** – AdWords, banner ads, etc...

The percentage of traffic from each of the first three sources will vary based on whether your product receives a lot of links from blogs and social media sites, or whether it's more search engine friendly.

If your site has a lot of clout with search engines you might find yourself receiving 95% of your traffic from organic search.

If you have a great story that people are talking about, you might find yourself with 95% of your traffic from incoming links.

Excluding advertising, which can vary depending on your campaign, a very general rule for the commerce-based websites I've been involved with have settled down to receiving around 1/3rd of their traffic from search engines, 1/3rd from incoming links, and 1/3rd from direct traffic.

Of course, the numbers will vary from month to month and site to site, but unless you have a reason to believe otherwise (such as creating a product where you expect to receive a large amount of buzz), an even split between the first three categories listed above provides a good estimate.

With this in mind, if we need 1,000 visitors at a price point of $200 to gross $1,000 per month, we need to bring in around 333 visitors per month via organic search. For safety let's round up to 500 visitors.

If we can rank high enough for enough keywords to garner 500 organic search engine visitors each month, it's a pretty good bet the other two categories (incoming links and direct traffic) will fall in line. Not a guarantee, but a reasonable assumption.

These guidelines apply a few months after launch. The first several months, your website traffic will be erratic and the most likely situation is that you will receive a trickle of traffic from incoming links and paid advertising, but not much else.

It takes a while to rank high in Google for a large quantity of terms – some say 12-18 months (this is known as the Google Sandbox and its existence is an ongoing debate). Even if there is no Google Sandbox, it will take a few months to begin ranking for enough terms to bring in a noticeable stream of traffic.

With that said, let's turn our eyes to a specific example.

The Power of Google
Let's take the example of a theoretical application: an inventory management system. It's a good example because it could conceivably sell for $200 at a conversion rate of 0.5%, so it fits with the assumptions we've made thus far.

At this point, we're looking for 500 visitors per month from organic traffic. Let's look at how we might determine if this is possible.

Imagine if you could peer into Google's database and see that every month, 5,000 people search for the term "inventory software." If you ranked #1 for this term you would receive a large amount of free traffic (close to 5,000 visitors per month).

Assuming conservatively that you would receive an additional 5,000 visitors from other sources, with a 0.5% conversion rate on a $200 price point, you're looking at $10,000 per month.

This niche seems like a no-brainer assuming it's not ultra-competitive.

Except for one problem: the major search engines don't make their search data public. As a result, there's no way to know for sure how many times per month a given term is searched for.

However, there are sources of data that are publicly available and, using a bit of gucoowork and proprietary algorithms, several tools offer reasonable approximations for monthly search counts.

This is the path we will follow; gauging demand for a product before you build it based on monthly Google searches for certain terms. We use Google since it provides decent research tools, and owns around 75% of the market[29].

I should mention that looking at search queries is only one way to gauge demand. If you have access to a group of people through a blog or a mailing list, a survey can be an excellent source of information. But assuming you don't have a large audience at your disposal, search engines are the best option. However, they are not fool-proof for determining if your product will fly.

---

[29] Varies based on locale

To get started we have to brainstorm a handful of terms as a starting point for our research.

Start at the Top of the List
Take out your list of warm niches you created at the start of this chapter.

Looking through the list of hobbies and occupations, choose the top 5 based purely on your interest or passion in those areas, ranking them in your order of interest. So you might have a list like:

- Comic Books (hobby)
- Web Designer (occupation)
- Wine Making (hobby)
- Doctor (occupation)
- Accountant (occupation)

The next step is to determine what kind of software each of these niches desperately needs. We'll do some of this research online, but the best place to start is with your contact for the niche (the person in the right-hand column).

Give this person a call and grill her on what pains her in the job or hobby that could be solved with software. You'll probably find at least a few ideas; everyone loves to talk about their daily woes, and especially about how awful their software is.

Next, we'll hit a few keyword tools to see if there are other product ideas that people are searching for that your contact didn't mention.

Before we begin, you'll also want to bring along that secret list of application ideas you keep tucked away. You know the one I'm talking about – we all have it, whether it's written down or not. The list of apps we've been meaning to build for years. Bring these along just for kicks.

Measuring Demand

The Micropreneur Methodology for measuring demand with search engines uses the following free tools:

- **Google AdWords Keyword Suggestion Tool**[30]
- **SEO Logs Keyword Difficulty Tool**[31]

Or the following tool which costs $97 (one-time fee):

- **Micro Niche Finder**[32] – The marketing for this tool is bad, but the tool itself is extremely powerful.

Before we delve into the approach, let's get a little background on keyword difficulty tools. Keyword difficulty tools can give us an estimate of the difficulty to rank for a term. Since this is an important and complex issue, let's look briefly at the three price points and capabilities of these tools.

The Three Tiers of Keyword Difficulty Tools

This section looks at some of the tools you can use to measure the difficulty of ranking for a particular keyword in Google.

I've used the SEO Logs Keyword Difficulty Tool for the past few years, but in recent months began using a pay tool called Micro Niche Finder that, in my experience, has provided more accurate information about keyword difficulty than any free tool I've found.

The Ideal Approach

The thing to keep in mind as we talk through these tools is that the only "right" way to determine keyword difficulty is to know Google's ranking algorithm. This is obviously a tightly

---

[30] https://adwords.google.com/select/KeywordToolExternal

[31] http://www.seologs.com/keyword-difficulty.html

[32] http://tinyurl.com/26xhld5

kept secret that Google isn't planning to share with us anytime soon.

However, even if we knew their algorithm, we know that it's changing constantly. Everything we are going to attempt below is an estimate of their algorithm. The question is: how close do you want your estimate to be (and how much are you willing to pay to get it)?

In the Beginning
In the beginning, the master metric of keyword difficulty was KEI, which stands for Keyword Effectiveness Index. The formula for KEI is:

number of searches per month / number of results

If you know anything about ranking in Google you'll know this is a hollow metric. While it worked pretty well 5+ years ago it's too simple to capture the intricacies of today's search engine algorithms.

The Next Step
The next step in the evolution was to begin to incorporate other factors such as how good the SEO is on a particular page you are trying to compete against. Some of the easiest factors to measure include how many pages in Google's index have your keyword in their HTML page title, and how many have links to them with your keyword in the link text.

Using some clever Google queries, you can manually research individual keywords using a spreadsheet, as described in this article:

http://www.internetbusinesspath.com/search-engine-optimization/day-5-evaluating-your-keyword-difficulty

This is a good approach, but time consuming and not feasible for evaluating multiple niches quickly. In addition, while it takes more factors into account than the free online tools, it will likely not be as accurate as any of the paid tools mentioned below.

The Alternative to a Spreadsheet
With that in mind, instead of a spreadsheet I recommend a keyword difficulty tool which will let our computers do the heavy lifting.

Through experience, I've grouped keyword difficulty tools into three buckets:

- **Free tools** (such as SEO Logs)
- **Pay tools** (such as Micro Niche Finder, which costs $97)
- **SEOmoz** ($79-229/month)

I realize it's odd that the third bucket is a single tool, but it's so far ahead of the others, it deserves its own category. Let's take a look at each type:

Type 1: Free
There are a few dozen free keyword difficulty tools on the web, but the vast majority of them are junk. Several of them crash when you run them, and some never return results.

The most popular tools are:

- **SEO Logs** – According to the site, this uses keyword saturation to determine its difficulty numbers. Essentially, it uses the number of results for the keyword in the major search engines.
- **SEO Chat** – No explanation of how it works.

The simplistic approach of the above tools implies they can provide ballpark estimates that should be taken with a grain of salt. If you are interested in more detailed data you should either use Micro Niche Finder or SEOmoz, or refer to the spreadsheet approach mentioned above.

The limitation with the above tools is the number of times you can query Google in a given second, minute, hour, or day. These free tools get hammered and as such are unable to run multiple detailed queries about every keyword.

A tool like SEOmoz requires you to enter your own Google API key, and Micro Niche Finder is a desktop app so your requests are not running from a centralized server.

This means you can query until your IP is blocked (this happens to me every couple weeks when using Micro Niche Finder), whereas if it ran from a central server they could never pull all of the detailed information they do for each keyword without getting blocked by Google.

Type 2: Pay Tool – Micro Niche Finder

Micro Niche Finder uses more advanced techniques such as the following Google queries:

- inanchor
- intitle
- inurl

The result is that it returns a better estimate of the strength of your competition.

The downside? It costs $97 (and the marketing for this product is really bad – very "late night TV"). But the tool is solid; I use it 3-5 times a week and have been doing so for the past 9+ months. It's been worth the one-time $97 given my usage.

Type 3: SEOmoz

The SEOmoz keyword difficulty tool is in a class of its own. It is a Rolls Royce to everyone else's Toyota.

There are detailed write-ups with screenshots that provide detailed information that you can read here:

- http://www.seomoz.org/blog/keyword-difficulty-tool-upgrade
- http://seogadget.co.uk/understanding-search-rankings-competitiveness/

This tool incorporates and weighs factors such as:

- # of results for a given keyphrase
- # of results in quotes
- PageRank of the top ranking pages/sites
- # of links pointing to the top ranking pages/sites
- Maximum bid price in the paid search results
- # of ads showing for a given query

The result is probably the most accurate view of keyword competition anywhere. The problem? You can only use it if you are an SEOmoz member, which costs $79/month for their least expensive plan.

Conclusion

There is no right or wrong answer; it's a question of how much you are willing to pay for the level of accuracy you want.

My recommendation is to use the spreadsheet approach *once* to learn the ins and outs of keyword difficulty checking and to get a feel for the process. Then you can either incorporate additional factors if you want more accuracy (including the SEO Logs results), or purchase a paid tool if you plan to do multiple searches over the course of time.

The Steps to Measuring Demand

We're going to look at two approaches for measuring demand: the free approach and the approach using Micro Niche Finder.

The Free Approach

Step 1: Google AdWords Keyword Tool

Visit https://adwords.google.com/select/KeywordToolExternal

Enter your main phrase, without quotes, into the Google AdWords Keyword Tool. Include synonyms, and run the search. Once the search results display, change the search type to "exact match." Run the search again.

Exact match limits your search to the exact phrase someone entered, not a variation of that phrase. For example, if someone searches on "blue running shoes" they will show up on a *broad match* for "blue," "running shoes," "blue running" and "blue running shoes." But they are an exact match only for the exact phrase they searched for: "blue running shoes."

The results you see are approximations of how many people search for this term, and related terms, each month. If you are going after global traffic, use the global column, for traffic in your own country, use the local column. This is not an exact count but it gives you a relative measure.

Using the formulas I discussed above, if you search on *billing software* you see that there are approx. 8,100 global monthly searches for the exact phrase "medical billing software." This is a healthy volume of searches.

The term "attorney billing software" has only 1,900 global searches per month. Is it a better market than "billing software"? Let's take a quick look:

Assuming you could rank #1 for this term in Google, you would likely receive about 50% of this 1,900 value. This is because, at the time of this writing, the AdWords Keyword Tool over-estimates search traffic. The rule of thumb is to take the value it shows and cut it in half.

Now we use the *Micropreneur Methodology*: we multiply that 50% value by 4 to get an approximate overall traffic if you ranked #1 for this keyword.

Why 4? Let's look:

- If you rank #1 for this generic keyword you will also rank highly for a number of long-tail keywords, which can easily bring in more traffic than a single main keyword. For safety sake, we multiply your total search engine traffic by 2.
- Since you will also have other streams of traffic coming to your site (remember the 1/3rd, 1/3rd, 1/3rd discussion above?), we can multiply 3,800 by 3 to get an approximation of all of your traffic, but to be safe let's multiply by 2.

So we can approximate that you might receive 3,800 visitors (1,900 x 0.5 x 2 x 2) per month if you ranked #1 for this term.

Assuming a $500 price point implies a fairly low conversion rate due to the high price and speed at which attorneys make technology decisions. If we assume 0.2%, you're looking at $3,800 per month in revenue.

It's not the next Facebook, but it's a good start. For a Micropreneur, this is a great market. For a bootstrapper, perhaps the first step in a billing software empire.

Step 2: Choose Keywords
Once you've chosen an anchor keyword like "attorney billing software" look at the tool results for other related keywords and track them in a text file. Keywords like "legal billing software" and "attorney invoicing software" qualify as related terms.

Step 3: SEO Logs Keyword Difficulty Tool
Visit http://www.seologs.com/keyword-difficulty.html.

Enter each keyword you pulled in steps 1 and 2 and enter them one at a time into this tool.

The score that comes back is a rough approximation (based on the number of search results returned in Google) of how hard it is to rank for this term. The lower the score, the better.

39 or below is good. 60 or above is bad. 40-59 is so-so.

"attorney billing software" (without the quotes) returns a 39. It should be easy to rank for.

"legal billing software" (without the quotes) returns a 45. This one is a bit harder.

Step 4: Sanity Check

Remember that this free tool is a pretty bad approximation, so our next step is to do a sanity check on what we've seen so far.

1. To do so, search Google for your keyword. In our case, "attorney billing software" (no quotes). Navigate to the first result in the list.
2. Look at the PageRank of this page using the Google Toolbar (if you don't have it, get it[33]). The PageRank for the #1 result is a 5. Ouch. That's going to hurt.
3. View the source of the page and look at the meta keywords and description. This page is optimized – this person knows what they are doing.
4. Enter the domain into Network Solutions Whois[34]. In this case the domain was registered in 1999. Double ouch. Older domains have more credibility in Google. This one's going to be tough to beat.
5. Finally, using the Google Toolbar, click on the PageRank meter and from the drop down list select "Backward Links." While this site only has 4 links, due to its age it has a lot of authority in Google.

It's hard to make a final judgment without looking at the sites ranked #2-5, but this site is going to be tough to beat. I would lean away from this niche based on the competition. The battle to the #1 spot is going to take 6-12 months to topple with SEO.

---

[33] toolbar.google.com

[34] http://www.networksolutions.com/whois/

There's actually another sanity check to be done here: I know from having worked with lawyers that they are resistant to new technology. This market would not only be difficult to SEO for, but getting lawyers to buy new software is extremely challenging. That alone may be enough to drive me away from this market.

The Micro Niche Finder Approach
Using Micro Niche Finder, the approach is a one-step process. Enter your keyword and search.

The results come back with a number of related keywords, the search count, ad cost and strength of competition (SOC) for each one.

For example, a search for "construction software" (without the quotes) provides a long list of related keywords with the relevant data. Here are the top 5 relevant results by search volume.

Note: You want the strength of SEO competition (SOC) to be low; under 100 is good. Over 1,000 is tough competition.

Keyword	Monthly Search Volume	Ad Cost ($)	SOC
project management software	301,000	10.72	69,500
construction software	14,800	6.36	2,970
project software	12,100	8.27	2,390
planning software	8,100	4.08	44,800
engineering software	6,600	2.58	3,430

There are a total of 200 results returned for this query, but the five above are a good sample.

The monthly search volume is simply the exact match results from the Google AdWords Keyword tool, but the value provided by Micro Niche Finder is its ability to create additional synonyms for your keywords, display the ad costs for each keyword, and the ease of retrieving the strength of the SEO competition for each keyword.

You can also retrieve the exact phrase count (how many pages are returned for this exact phrase in Google), and retrieve commercial intent, which attempts to gauge how likely someone is to buy something when they search on this keyword.

Given the above results, we see that *project management software* appears at the top of the list when ordered by monthly search volume. This term appears when searching on construction software because Micro Niche Finder is good at finding related, though not identical keyphrases to the term you enter.

Project management software receives a lot of monthly searches, but the SEO competition is unbelievably high. I would expect to work for 1-2 years before ranking on the first page of Google for this term.

You can see from the comparison that MNF provides everything in one fell swoop, while the AdWords Keyword Tool approach requires a bit more legwork. I would still do a sanity check on the top rankings before moving forward, but with MNF you get the end result faster.

Testing an Idea for Under $100

Estimating demand with a keyword tool is one thing, but watching the behavior of real website visitors as they click through your website, browse, and try or buy is a completely different experience. This section looks at an approach for running a final test on your product idea before investing hundreds of hours into building it.

Background

Keyword tools are flawed.

They're the best information we have, but they're nothing more than estimates of search traffic based on extrapolated data. But there is an approach that can give us the exact number of Google searches performed for a given keyword in a given timeframe.

The approach is to place an exact match AdWords ad (using quotations around the keyword) and bid high enough to ensure your ad is on the first page. Every time the term is searched for, your ad will appear. At any given time, you can go into your AdWords console and see how many times the search has been performed.

Of course, this isn't free – you'll pay every time someone clicks your ad. But the cost involved, typically $.10-$1.00 per click, is low enough that it's worth exploring this approach before investing time to build your product.

The Benefits of AdWords

Beyond being able to verify search counts, the benefits of AdWords for the testing approach we discuss below are numerous:

- There is no minimum investment, unlike most forms of advertising
- You can turn it on and off instantly, unlike SEO and other advertising
- It's relatively inexpensive

As such, AdWords is an ideal tool for testing a product idea. Testing an idea is the next step after narrowing from say, the 20 niches you wrote down earlier in this chapter, to 1-4 product ideas you narrowed to in the last section using keyword tools.

Since we know the data used in the above discussion is relatively accurate, what we'll cover in this lesson will test those assumptions further. This test can be run for anywhere between $50 and $500 depending on the cost of AdWords in your niche and how far you want to take it.

The Approach

We're going to look at an approach to testing your market called the *Mini Sales Site*.

I developed this approach a few years ago after reading the 4-Hour Workweek, realizing that the author's testing approach could be re-purposed from information and physical product testing to software products.

Since then, a similar approach has been defined by the *Lean Startup Methodology*. I take it as a sign that we're both on the right track.

The Mini Sales Site

The idea behind this approach is that if you ask visitors whether or not they would buy your product, you will wind up with inaccurate data. The only way you know if someone would try or buy your product is if they think they are really trying or buying it when they visit your sales site.

Since we don't want to build a complete sales site to run this test, we use a mini sales site which is a stripped down version of the same.

The mini sales site approach works best if you are selling a downloadable or web-based (SaaS) application.

The steps for setting it up are as follows:

1. From your short list of product options, choose the idea that is most interesting to you.
2. Setup a *Mini Sales Site* that includes two or three pages (see chapter 4 for more details on building these pages):

- o Home
- o Product Tour (optional)
- o Pricing & Sign-up

3. Your Home page and Tour page will contain screen shots, a feature list and full product information, along with a call to action to try/buy your product.
4. If your product is downloadable and costs under $40, try to get people to click a "buy now" button on your Pricing & Sign-up page.
5. If your product is downloadable and more than $40, try to get visitors to click a "download a free trial" button on your Pricing & Sign-up page.
6. If your product is a SaaS or mobile application, try to get visitors to click a "buy now" button on your Pricing & Sign-up page.
7. Create an AdWords campaign and send targeted traffic to your site.
8. When someone clicks "Try it" or "Buy Now", track conversions using Google AdWords and notify the prospect that your product is still in development. Ask for their email address so you can notify them when you launch. You may get their email, and you may not. Either way, you should have the conversion goal programmed into AdWords so you know which keyword converted, and you'll be able to see how much money you spent for each conversion.

You may have qualms about this approach, thinking you're misleading prospects. If you feel bad about presenting your product as complete when it's not, include a "Coming soon" emblem somewhere on your pages.

In addition, realize that most people on the web are browsing. If a customer is not interested in your product they will know it right away and they will never click "try" or "buy." If they *are* interested and it fits their needs, odds are good they're going to be interested a few months down the line when you launch. So allowing them to sign up for a launch notification will likely be a desired benefit for them.

In the meantime you get to obtain metrics on actual searches performed for your keywords, which keywords convert, and what your expected conversion rate will be.

After sending 100-200 visitors to your site, look at the numbers of "trials" or "purchases." Assume you will convert between 2% and 5% of people who clicked "try now" or "download free trial." Assume 40% of the people who clicked "buy now" would have completed the purchase.

When Not to Use This Approach
In general, this approach will not work if you are planning to build a social networking or social media site, or any other product that's reliant on a network effect. With these types of sites you can't test the idea until you try it out with a full-blown marketing effort.

But if you're selling a niche downloadable, mobile or web-based (SaaS) application this approach will work.

The Components
- **Screenshots** – For application screen shots, you can build them yourself or pay a designer for mockups – you only need 2-3 screens and they never have to be built into HTML. A designer should be able to create a design and 2-3 mock-ups of your key screens for a few hundred dollars or less.
- **Sales Copy** – We discuss sales copy in chapter 4.
- **AdWords Setup and Tracking Conversions** – For detailed information on setting up an AdWords campaign and tracking conversions through AdWords, see the Micropreneur Academy[35] or the *Ultimate Guide to Google AdWords*[36].

---

[35] www.Micropreneur.com

Case Study: College Coach Finder

I've been planning to test a new product idea this fall, when fourth-year high school athletes around the country begin to search for colleges. You'd be surprised to hear that there are only a few online resources to help high school athletes find a school that includes a specific sport, and then allows them to contact the coach of that sport.

I researched this idea and came across a pristine data set of the information needed to build a product that could bridge this gap. The problem: the data costs several thousand dollars per year to license.

If the idea is a success the licensing fee will be a small price to pay, but if it fails it will be a large up-front expense that should have been avoided.

In preparation for the college search "season" which begins in October, I've had my designers prepare comps for a Mini Sales Site that they will build into HTML and I will test using the methods mentioned above.

The comps are still in draft form, but you can see them on the next two pages.

---

[36] http://tinyurl.com/26l4yr3

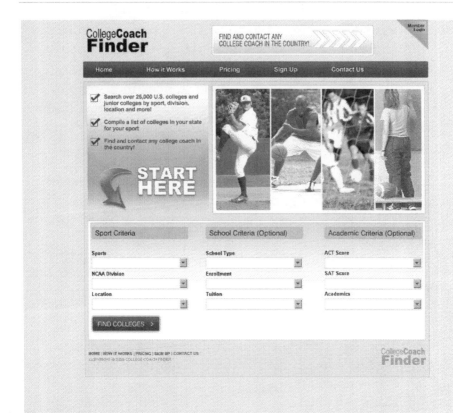

Home Page

Sign Up Page

The total cost for the design and HTML was less than $300.

By driving traffic using AdWords and tracking how many website visitors click the "search" button and how many click the "sign up" button I will gain valuable insight into the potential success of this idea before spending literally thousands of dollars building it.

Conclusion

Using the approaches above will require you to invest some time and money. But realize that if you invest 8 hours now and the test works, you will have confidence that will keep you going through the next 4 months of development. If it fails miserably, you're saving yourself hundreds of hours and potentially thousands of dollars building a product no one wants.

While this approach cannot provide you with 100% certainty that your idea will succeed or fail, it forces you to take the next step towards launching your product.

Chapter 3

Your Product

The Product Success Triangle

The success of your product will depend on three things:
product, market and execution, which together make up what I
call the *Product Success Triangle.*

- **Product** - Your product has to be good
- **Market** - You need a group of people willing to pay
  money for it
- **Execution** – You have to market, sell, and support it

In the paradigm above, your product is one-third of the
equation. This is far from the hefty weight most developers
place on the product. Speak with most new developer-
entrepreneurs and you'll get the impression that the product is
99% of the equation.

But a brilliant product with no market or execution is dead. A
mediocre product with brilliant marketing and execution will
make you money.

You should aim to master all three in the long-term but at the
start, place emphasis on the latter two to determine if the idea
will fly. Once you know you have a market and can execute,

then you can improve your product. For this reason this book focuses on the latter two steps.

This is also the reason why hiring out construction of your product is a viable option; it doesn't have to be the masterpiece you picture in your mind in order to be successful.

I realize this is hard to accept. As developers we think the code is the most important part. So although I'm not going to harp on "hiring it out" too much, it's a topic we need to investigate so you can decide for yourself.

Let's take a look at the difference between building your product, and hiring out some of the development.

Building It

You love writing software, so building will be your first choice. Let's take a look at some ballpark numbers to give you an idea of how much time you'll need to get your product off the ground.

There are a million ways to estimate software projects. Here is a good way to get an order of magnitude estimate:

- Create a site map (for websites) or list of screens (for desktop apps).
- Sketch out how each page will look using pen and paper. This should take about 2 minutes per page. You don't have to sketch out all the pages or even capture all the functionality; you're simply trying to get an idea about the complexity of each page.
- Estimate 4-12 hours per page depending on complexity.
- Add 10-20 hours for DB design depending on complexity.
- Estimate back-end functionality such as credit card processing, PayPal integration, or scheduled tasks. Add 10-40 hours each, depending on your experience.
- Add it up.

As a rule of thumb, your path to 1.0 should fall between 200 and 400 hours.

If you're under 200, it's a good sign, but take a second look at whether you are offering enough functionality to differentiate yourself from the competition, or if you are really building a "tool" rather than a full-blown application. The difference is that you'll have a tough time charging people to use a tool, while an application will provide real value and bring in revenue.

If you're over 400 hours, take a serious look at eliminating functionality to shorten your time to launch. This is the most common mistake I've seen with 1.0 products – too many features and too many months between the start of development and launch.

The sales website, documentation, marketing, and everything else will be 100-200 hours.

If you're coding in your spare time, it will be a stretch to get 15 hours of productive work in per week. In addition, your productivity will be lower than during the day since you'll be working in 2 hour blocks and will be tired from your day job. I've done it – it's not easy.

At 15 hours per week, 300 hours means 20 weeks of your free time, or 4-1/2 months. At 550 hours you're looking at 8-1/2 months. Think about how much time that is – it's pretty incredible to think about spending most evenings and weekends for the next 8 months building a product and generating no revenue during that time span.

Do You Have the Time?
Before you choose this option you need to ask yourself if you can commit most of your spare time for the next 4-1/2 to 8-1/2 months to building your application. Also think about talking to your spouse or significant other before making this decision.

Remember that if you spend time building this product and later decide to scrap it, you've essentially wasted the hours you spent working on it.

Ask yourself if you have confidence in your product idea and in your ability to market it. We'll show you how to answer both of those questions in the next few lessons.

Compared to hiring out, building your own application is more likely to lead to burnout and an early decision to quit. If you have a few thousand dollars set aside, you should consider hiring out development. If the only reason you're not going down this path is because you want to be in control of the code, then you need to seriously re-think whether or not you can let that go. Letting it go and stepping away from the code will increase your chance of launching.

However, if you have no money and a lot of time on your hands, then building your own product is a great option.

One final note: if you could scrape together an additional 10 hours per week for a total of 25 hours of development per week, your time to launch would drop to less than 3 months @ 300 hours.

If you are dedicated to your product idea and can afford it in the short term, you may want to think about working 4 days per week with the idea that in the future, you will replace the lost income with product revenue.

Hiring It Out
Hiring someone to build your software is a good middle ground, as it allows you some control over the technical aspects of your product without sucking the coding life from your veins.

The biggest hurdle when deciding whether to hire someone to build your software is that you think you can build software better than the next person.

You don't have to admit this to anyone, but every good developer I know thinks his/her code is the best code out there, and that by hiring it out they will receive a poorly-written product. If you're going to hire out your software construction:

> *You have to get over your desire to write the software yourself.*

You do. You have to accept the fact that the code is not going to be in exactly your style, and it may not be as good as if you build it yourself.

However, once you find a good developer you won't believe how good someone else's code can be. And depending on if you're open to offshoring development, you could have your entire application developed for under $3,000 (200 hours @ $15/hour for a Senior PHP Developer).

You can also hire out your sales site design and HTML development which will cost $500-1,500 and save you another 50 hours.

The advantage of hiring this out is it gives you time to write copy, write documentation, focus on SEO, set up PPC advertising, hook up payment processing, and the hundred other things you'll need to get this product off the ground. You can focus on the second two facets of the success pyramid.

And think about it...a lot of people can build a good invoicing application.

But how many can work the necessary marketing angles, form partnerships, create a profitable pay per click campaign, and build a compelling sales site? Finding someone who can execute on these is much more difficult (and more expensive) than finding a developer who can build your application.

With this in mind, let's take a swing at all of the costs involved with this approach:

- The graphic design and HTML will run from $500-$1,500 if you offshore. Handling it in the U.S. will cost $2,000-6,000.
- Two months of development (a safe estimate when hiring someone to build a small product from scratch) will run $12k-$20k here in the states, or around $6k if you offshore.
- Total you're looking at $14k-$26k in the states, $6.5k-7.5k if you offshore. These are very rough numbers based on a typical small startup product requiring two months of development.

If you have some basic project management skills and can scrape $7k together, you can save yourself a few hundred hours of coding, get to market faster, and focus more time on marketing.

This is the last time I will mention this option in this book. I realize most readers will not entertain this option and that's okay. But I wanted to show it to you since it has significant benefits and many developers I've worked with have found success using this approach.

How to Price Your Product

Determining your price is one of the most challenging aspects of launching a product. You've likely read articles on the subject before, and you're likely still confused about how to determine the best price for your product.

In this section we discuss specific dollar amounts you'll want to keep in mind as you hone in on a price. We'll also look at a 12-step process for determining your optimal pricing structure.

General Guidelines for Pricing

In researching this topic I read no less than 25 articles, blog posts and PDFs relating to software pricing. Not one provided even a loose range for the amount you should consider charging for a product. I'm going to break that mold.

Each of the prices mentioned below is a ballpark number and will vary considerably based on your market specifics, but let them serve as a general guideline of the top end of each market segment. Keep in mind I'm only referring to online sales here – selling on the internet without a sales person or in-person visit. Large software firms who can afford staffs of sales people can charge much more than the numbers provided here.

For consumer products dealing with hobbies (i.e., products that aren't going to make or save someone money), you're going to have a tough time charging more than $29 fixed-price or $14/month.

For consumer products that will make or save someone a tangible amount of money you're going to top out around $49 or $19/month.

For small businesses you're going to top out around $400 or $99/month unless you solve a serious pain.

For larger businesses your top end will be around $1,000[37] or $199/month unless you solve a serious pain.

Finding Your Price

If you've ever purchased a home you may have gone through the appraisal process. When an appraiser determines the value of a home they can use one or more of the following methods:

---

[37] See Joel Spolsky's reasoning for background on this $1,000 figure: http://www.joelonsoftware.com/articles/CamelsandRubberDuckies.html

1. **Comparable Sales in the Area** – Looks at similar homes that have recently sold in the same area
2. **Replacement Value** – Looks at what it would cost to re-build the structure if it was destroyed
3. **Income Approach** – Looks at market rent and using a multiplier determines how much the house would be worth to an investor.

In residential appraisals, the Comparable Sales approach is much more prominent. However, in investor real estate you will see appraisals with two or three of the approaches merged into a single number.

Arriving at your core price requires the same approach; we're going to look at a few methods for determining a good price and merge the results.

The steps for finding your first cut at a purchase price are:

1. **Know your market.** The first step is to get a sense of your market and of the price it will bear, using the *General Guidelines for Pricing* listed above. You also need to find out how software is typically purchased by your buyers, how they will pay for it, and how much they can purchase without approval.
2. **Ask yourself.** When 37Signals determines pricing for a new product[38] they ask themselves the following two questions:
   a. What would we pay?
   b. What numbers *feel* right?
3. **Look at your competition**. If you have competition this step is easy. With little or no competition you'll need to compare to similar markets. Writing inventory software for small businesses? Look at invoicing or accounting software for small businesses.

---

[38] http://www.37signals.com/svn/posts/1287-ask-37signals-how-did-you-come-up-with-pricing-for-your-products

4. **Determine your product's value.** If your software saves your prospect 5 hours per month and you can monetize their time at $25/hour you will save them $125 per month. You won't be able to charge more than this figure, but you can use this as a top-end of your potential price.

5. **Combine.** Use the numbers from steps 2-4 to determine the optimal price range for your product. Ideally you want the high end of your range to be 4x your low end.

6. **Lean towards higher pricing.** Developers tend to undervalue their software, and think that lower prices will result in higher sales. This is typically not the case.

7. **Use three tiers.** There is no single best price for your product, so shoot for multiple price points. Use the low end of your range as your lowest tier price. Multiply by 2 for your middle tier, and multiply your middle tier by 2 for the top tier.

8. **End in 7, 8 or 9.** It's stupid, but it works. Make each of your three prices (the dollar column) end in a 7, 8 or 9 and be sure they all end with the same number.

9. **Determine the benefits of each tier.** For each tier, based on your knowledge of your market, decide which metric(s) will increase as you step up the tiers (invoices sent, disk space, processing power?). Ensure that as your price doubles from tier to tier, you provide more than double the benefit.

10. **Add Support.** If you charge a one-time fee for your software, seriously consider charging 20% of that fee annually for support and product upgrades. Failing to charge a yearly software maintenance fee will cut into your profit margin every single time you speak with a customer.

11. **Alternate method for calculating recurring payments.** If you have a recurring monthly fee and for some reason it's easier to determine a fixed-price for your type of software (perhaps there are no competitors

with recurring fees), take the fixed-price and divide by 12 for your highest tier.

12. **Test.** Try the price testing techniques mentioned below. Don't be confident in your numbers until you've tested them.

How to Test Pricing

Human behavior is irrational. This means no one knows the right pricing structure for your product. Instead of finding a price point and latching onto it for eternity, you should test your pricing to determine how far you can push it.

And your approach to price testing depends on your sales cycle.

Testing is simple if you have a constant flood of new traffic and you make enough sales that you can run a 1-3 day test and see the results. With a more expensive product it's more complex, since sales cycles can be a few months or more and you stand a higher possibility that existing customers will find out about your price tests.

Here are recommended approaches for price testing based on the duration of your sales cycle:

- If your sales cycle is less than 1 week, change your pricing without notifying anyone. Leave it running for 1-2 weeks, and compare your results.
- If your sales cycle is longer than 1 week use one of the following techniques:
  - Increase your price when you launch a new version and offer the old price for 7 days to anyone on your mailing list. This will create a quick influx of sales, and you'll get away with raising your price because new prospects will have never seen the old one. Then, after a few weeks (depending on how many sales you make during a given period), determine if revenue has

increased with the higher price. If not, drop it back to its previous level.

o Decrease your price and watch if revenue increases (again, you have to wait for a few weeks depending on how many copies you typically sell in a week). You can move back to the old pricing a week or two later if sales do not increase. If you receive emails from existing customers, offer to refund the difference for them.

Product Types

Six major product types are described below, including the typical pricing structure, benefits, downsides and when to use each.

Type #1 – Hosted Web Applications

These days hosted web applications are called Software as a Service applications (SaaS), but you may know them by their previous name, ASP Applications (for Application Service Provider), or the new name the media seems to be misusing more and more, "Cloud-based Applications."

Most new business or productivity applications are hosted web applications. Examples abound, but here are some of the more popular options:

- **FreshBooks**[39] (hosted invoicing)
- **Basecamp**[40] (hosted project management software)
- **FogBugz on Demand**[41] (hosted bug tracking / project management)

---

[39] www.freshbooks.com

[40] basecamphq.com

[41] www.fogcreek.com/FogBugz/

Pricing Structure
- Typically a monthly or annual recurring fee

Benefits for the Entrepreneur
- Steady, recurring revenue
- Support is much easier than software installed on a user's machine since you are in control of every aspect of the deployment and are only maintaining a single version of the application
- Documentation can be updated as you add features
- Customer feedback can be incorporated immediately into the product, thus providing incremental improvements on a shorter release schedule

Benefits for the Customer
- Customers do not make a large, up-front capital investment to pay for software licenses
- Customers do not have to maintain their own servers, install or upgrade software, or open a shared hosting account
- Upgrades are free, seamless, and require no effort on the part of the customer
- Customers can try your product with little effort

The Downside
- Developing for the web can be challenging and you have to learn a number of technologies to build an application (HTML/CSS/AJAX/JS/Server Side Code)
- Browser compatibility issues can be cumbersome, especially with browser market share becoming more and more splintered
- Some customers, typically enterprise clients, will not allow their data to live outside of company walls and thus will not use hosted web applications
- It requires you to maintain a 24/7 uptime hosting solution, plus security and backups

When to Use

When thinking about a new application aimed at businesses, start with the position of a hosted web application. The ease of support, ease of adoption, and recurring revenue model are major advantages.

Joel Spolsky, CEO of Fog Creek Software[42], said in an interview on Venture Voice[43] that if he were starting his company today he would not build a downloadable version of their flagship product, FogBugz.

For hosted applications the question is not "when to use" it's "when *not* to use."

Don't use a hosted web application if:

- You are targeting a specific community of people such as iPhone or Facebook users.
- You're targeting enterprise clients who will want their data to live inside their own walls
- Your user interface has complex needs that an AJAX/DHTML interface cannot support
- Your application needs direct hard drive access or peripheral access that require a desktop application

Type #2 – Downloadable Web Applications

Downloadable web applications serve a single purpose: to allow customers to use your web application but never lose control of their data.

Given the need for some companies to keep data inside their walls, or the need for them to guarantee 24/7/365 uptime means there is a market for downloadable web applications.

---

[42] www.fogcreek.com

[43] www.venturevoice.com

Downloadable web applications need to be installed only by someone with a moderate level of technical competence. This restriction eliminates 99.9% of the people in the world.

Pricing Structure

- One-time fee, but can include an annual support fee, typically around 20% of the purchase price
- Though rare, I've seen application leasing and rentals to eliminate the large up-front fee. You should consider building anti-piracy into your application if you want to pursue this avenue. It should allow you to remotely kill the application should the purchaser stop paying their lease or rental.

Benefits for the Entrepreneur

- No need to maintain a hosting infrastructure
- Typically the purchase price is received in a lump sum so one-time revenue is high compared with hosted solutions

Benefits for the Customer

- Customers maintain control of their data
- Customers can customize your application including the design or functionality, and integrate it with their own website or web applications

The Downside

- Support is a burden since every customer's server is different
- One-time, rather than recurring licensing fees
- Customers have to come up with a large amount of up-front capital to pay for software licenses
- Customers have to be technical to maintain their own servers so your market is smaller than with a hosted web application
- Upgrades are cumbersome, especially in cases where the customer has not upgraded for several versions

- If you have never developed for the web, the development environment can be challenging
- Browser compatibility issues can be cumbersome, especially with browser market share becoming more and more splintered
- Your target audience is fragmented based on the server side code you use to build your application. In other words, you have Windows users, Linux users, OS X and Unix users.
- Keeping track of customers who have purchased software maintenance and when it is due can be an additional burden.

When to Use
- When you're targeting enterprise clients or clients who want to maintain control of their own data
- When you're targeting software/web developers who want control to customize or integrate with your application in ways that can't be accomplished through building an API

Type #3 – Desktop Applications
Over the past 10 years, the trend of moving away from desktop applications and onto the web is obvious. New web applications are launched daily, and desktop applications are getting rarer as time goes on

But there is still a thriving need for desktop applications in several areas, including but not limited to audio and video editing, virus scanning, photo and document editing, and graphic design.

Pricing Structure
- One-time fee, but can include an annual support fee of around 20% of the purchase price

Benefits for the Entrepreneur
- No need to maintain hosting infrastructure

- The purchase price is received in a lump sum so one-time revenue is high
- No browser compatibility issues since it does not run in the browser

Benefits for the Customer

- Customers maintain control of their own data
- The user interface can be superior to a web application

The Downside

- Support is a burden since every customer's desktop is different
- One-time as opposed to recurring licensing fees
- Customers have to come up with a large amount of up-front capital to pay for software licenses
- Upgrades are cumbersome for your customer and create a support burden for you
- While you don't have browser compatibility issues, you have a more complex decision regarding whether to support multiple operating systems such as Windows, Linux, Mac, etc...
- Keeping track of customers who have purchased software maintenance and when it is due can be an additional burden

When to Use

- When your application has complexities that an AJAX/DHTML interface cannot support
- When your application needs direct hard drive or peripheral access that requires code to execute locally. Unless this is a core component of your application, you should consider building this functionality as a downloadable extension to a web application to help alleviate support for multiple operating systems.

Type #4 – Mobile Applications

Mobile applications run on cell phones, PDAs, MP3 players, and Smart Phones. This umbrella includes applications that run on any mobile operating system such as the iPhone, Windows Mobile, PalmOS, Google's Android OS, and a plethora of cell phone operating systems.

Mobile applications are a big topic right now as companies scramble for a land-grab in the iPhone application space. In the first 4 months after the iPhone launched, its application store it saw 10,000 apps developed by third-party developers.

Mobile applications are a market unto themselves much like web or desktop apps, with some projections putting the mobile app market at 100 million users by 2013[44].

Pricing Structure
- One-time fee
- One-time fee with a tie in to a recurring service
- Free. Many mobile applications are free to end users since they serve as additional means to access a hosted web application

Benefits for the Entrepreneur
- Often your audience has a single place where they can buy applications (such as through iTunes or their cell carrier's website) so there is high likelihood that users will accidentally discover your application
- The space is relatively new, so there is less competition than on the web or the desktop

Benefits for the Customer
- The convenience of having your application at their fingertips anytime

---

[44] http://news.softpedia.com/news/100-Million-Mobile-Users-to-Access-App-Stores-by-2013-107747.shtml

The Downside
- If you are not a mobile app developer you will have to learn an entirely new paradigm (or hire someone who already knows it)
- Getting your application into a cell carrier's catalog can be fraught with red-tape and can take weeks or months. It might even be denied outright.
- Phones have limited RAM and processing resources, limiting what you can do in an application. As an example, the iPhone 3G has a 412MHz CPU and 128MB of RAM.
- You will have to decide which platform to target – for the most part each one requires different development technologies

When to Use
- When you want to extend an existing web or desktop application by adding mobile capabilities
- When you have an application targeted specifically towards the mobile crowd

Type #5 – Third-Party Plug-ins

There are hundreds, if not thousands, of third party platforms on the web. Websites and applications such as Facebook, MySpace, WordPress, DotNetNuke, and SalesForce.com offer APIs and application platforms where you can build a product and have a group of users discover it through the platform's marketplace with little or no marketing effort on your part.

Developers have responded to many plug-in platforms in force, one example is the more than 77,000 Facebook apps developed in its first year of existence.

Here is a quick rundown of the potential market sizes for the largest platforms based on the most recent numbers I could track down:

- Facebook – over 500 million active users

- MySpace – over 125 million users
- SalesForce.com – over 1.5 million paying subscribers

Pricing Structure
- In the consumer space, applications are free and typically earn revenue through advertising, affiliate links, or driving traffic to a specific website where users can be monetized
- In the enterprise space (such as SalesForce.com) applications may have an up-front or recurring cost

Benefits for the Entrepreneur
- These platforms tend to have a high adoption rate for new plug-ins
- If you design your application correctly, you can achieve exponential growth using viral marketing since the social platforms tend to have a high network effect
- Often your audience has a single place where they can acquire applications (such as the Facebook Application Directory or Salesforce AppExchange) so there is more likelihood your application will be discovered accidentally than with an application on the open internet
- The space is relatively new so there is less competition than with web or desktop apps

Benefits for the Customer
- Convenience of new features and functionality without relying on the platform providers to build them
- Many plug-ins are free

The Downside
- Gold-rush mentality and dubious monetization methods means few applications ever make money
- Plugging functionality holes in the application of a major vendor will eventually backfire should the vendor incorporate your functionality into the main application

When to Use

- When you want to extend an existing web or desktop application by making it easy for platform users to add your application's capabilities
- When you have a product idea that's targeted towards a demographic that resides on a particular platform

Type #6 – Community Websites

Though not a conventional "cash for software" arrangement, community websites such as social networks, forums, social bookmarking tools, file sharing or photo sharing sites can not only be fun projects to build, but fun to market since the press is currently enamored with this market segment.

Community websites are the type of product most likely to wind up on the cover of *Fast Company* or *Inc.* since they grow so quickly and everyone can participate and understand how they work.

Though not typical sites for Micropreneurs or bootstrappers, these sites have the potential to grow very quickly and provide a fun ride for someone interested in raising funding and hiring employees.

Pricing Structure

- Community websites are most often ad-supported, but paid membership websites are becoming more common

Benefits for the Entrepreneur

- Fun, interesting projects to build, launch and market
- They have the "cocktail party" factor; when you tell someone you sell invoicing software they often have a sudden need to refill their drink, but telling someone you run a social network for lizard trainers can make you a quazi-celebrity

The Downside
- Difficult to get off the ground – much riskier than building and selling software
- Requires knowledge of community building
- Managing a community during early growth is very difficult to do by yourself

When to Use
- If you have a way to target potential customers for little or no money, such as a mailing list or blog
- If you have a good handle on viral marketing
- If you are interested in exploring the "go-big" style of startup. Most community sites are only financially viable with millions of page views per month.

Conclusion

The decision of pricing, whether to build or hire out, and which product type to build will have critical impact on how quickly you can make it to market, the size of your market, and how many copies you can sell.

Secondary only to your niche itself, these decisions must be decided on with the needs of your market in mind.

Chapter 4

Building a Killer Sales Website

Building a website that converts visitors to buyers is not done by accident. Most developers think that because they know HTML, they can build a website that will make people want to buy their product.

Unfortunately, there's more to it than most people realize.

The Sales Funnel

Sales funnels are mentioned in just about every book on selling, and they're especially handy when describing the online selling process.

The idea behind the sales funnel is that there are several steps between someone surfing the internet and buying your product.

1. First, that person must **see your URL**. This may be a link in a blog, a banner ad, a write-up on TechCrunch, an AdWords ad, or a link in a forum.
2. Second, they must click the link and **become a site visitor**.
3. Next, they must be interested enough to stick around for more than a few seconds; long enough to read your sales copy, watch your video demo, try your product

demo, and potentially provide you with their email address. At this point they have "raised their hand" as a potential customer and they **become a prospect**.

4. Finally, they must be convinced that your product is going to solve their problem for the right price, and they must make the purchase. Here they **become a buyer**.

At each step you will lose the majority of the group:

- Most people surfing the web will never see your URL
- Most people who see your URL will not click on it
- Most people who click on it will not be interested in your site long enough to become a prospect
- Most prospects will not buy your product

This process of starting with a large group and slowly whittling down to a small number of buyers is called the sales funnel, and it's shown in the figure below:

Something to notice: the chance of someone coming all the way from seeing your URL to becoming a buyer is small. The chance of them doing it on their first visit is almost zero.

After you launch your website you will need to test different approaches, copy, buttons and bonuses for each of the steps shown in the sales funnel to improve and hone them for maximum benefit. For example:

1. You will spend time making sure more people see your URL (getting written up in blogs, testing and increasing advertising that works, monitoring forums and offering your product as a solution, etc...)
2. You need to spend time turning browsers into prospects, meaning you need to engage them with your content, and convince them that they stand to gain by providing you with their email address
3. You need to spend time nurturing an ongoing relationship with your prospects to turn more of them into buyers, as well as honing your website sales pitch to increase your sales conversion rate

Every stage of your sales funnel is crucial to the process and you will have to devote time to optimizing each.

Here's an interesting fact to ponder:

If your website receives 1,000 visitors per month and you have a 1% sales conversion rate you are selling 10 copies of your product each month.

To increase sales by 1 copy each month (10%) you will need to do one of the following:

- Generate 100 more visitors to your website
- Increase your conversion rate by 0.1%

Which do you think is more difficult? Answer: the first.

Although common wisdom is to focus on traffic, the best internet marketers realize that increasing conversion rates for existing website visitors can yield a better return on investment.

Don't Plan to Sell to a Customer on Their First Visit

The first rule of sales websites is that the most common approach is wrong. That is:

> *You shouldn't plan to sell to a customer on their first visit*

This likely goes against many of the small software company sales website you've come across. It also may go against what you've seen on some of the more successful sales websites you've encountered (SourceGear Vault[45], FogBugz[46], and Basecamp[47]).

Think about the difference between the three websites I listed above and your sales website. What do those three have that yours doesn't?

The answer is: an audience of readers who will return again and again, perusing and thinking about the product until it's embedded in their brain. After this kind of exposure, it will always be their first choice should they ever need source control, bug tracking, or project management software.

Judging by the high profile websites we see, your image of the sales process might go something like this:

---

[45] www.sourcegear.com/vault/

[46] www.fogcreek.com/FogBugz/

[47] basecamphq.com

1. A person hears about your product on a blog and clicks through to your website.
2. Your product fits the visitor perfectly and they fumble for their wallet as they click to your checkout page, completing the purchase a minute or two after they first land on your website.

This is by far the exception.

In chapter 2 we talked about conversion rates and I mentioned that typical conversion rates are between 0.5% and 4% depending on your price range and customer base. What that means is that for every 1,000 website visitors, between 960 and 995 will show up and leave without doing a thing.

If you're paying 50 cents per click for your traffic, it can become expensive rather quickly. Not only that, but it's not cost effective if the price of acquiring a customer is higher than your product purchase price.

Visitors who become buyers typically return numerous times to your site over the course of several days or weeks, depending on the length of your sales cycle.

The reality of the sales process is closer to the following:

1. Five minutes before a meeting, a potential customer performs a Google search for a term related to your product.
2. They see your Google AdWords ad next to their search results. They click through to your website. You are charged 50 cents.
3. The visitor looks around; skipping large blocks of text, scanning images, watching the first 30 seconds of your video demo and zipping through your pricing page.
4. After making a mental note to come back to your site they close the browser and run off to their meeting, never to return again.

You will never be able to keep this person from being in a hurry. And you won't be able to force them to read your content.

But you *can* help them come back.

The Number One Goal of Your Website
Your number one goal, even beyond selling your product, is turning browsers into prospects. A prospect is someone who has expressed at least a small amount of interest in your product. On the web, this is typically achieved by asking someone to provide their email addresses.

Convincing someone to give you their email address is much easier than convincing them to buy your product. Once you have an email address, you have the chance to begin building a relationship with the customer, as well as to gently remind them, through relevant emails, to return to your website.

In order for someone to provide you with their email address you must do three things:

1. **Establish Trust** – Your visitor must believe that you aren't going to spam them, sell their email address, or send offers for V1@gra.
2. **Establish Relevance** – Your visitor must believe that your product is relevant to their need and that anything you send to them via email will be relevant.
3. **Establish a Reward** – We are predictable creatures. Offering something in exchange for an email address is guaranteed to work better than offering nothing. On DotNetInvoice.com I had an email sign-up form where people could receive email updates on our product. We received 3 sign-ups in 8 months. I switched to offering a chance to win a free copy of DotNetInvoice...30 sign-ups in a month. There's still room for improvement, but it's headed in the right direction. Now, when I send out the winner's announcement I'm going to include a small

snippet about the new features available in our latest version. The best rewards are: a contest, a relevant four- or five- day email course, a relevant white paper, or a webinar.

We'll talk more about building your mailing list later in this chapter, for now realize that your mailing list is crucial to your success.

Customer Profiles

Before you begin architecting your sales website, you need to understand what goes on inside your typical customer's head. From this stage, even before we've conceived any concrete details about your website, you need to think like a potential customer.

Your goal should be to understand what your ideal customer wants to find on your website, what they want to find in your product, and what triggers will make them buy.

To begin, imagine your ideal customer:

- Are they married?
- Do they have kids?
- How do they get to work?
- Do they work in an office? On a construction site? Driving a truck?
- How old are they?
- What kind of car do they drive?
- Do they watch TV? Surf the web? Listen to music?

Now imagine how your ideal customer feels when they arrive at your website:

- What do they want to find there?
- What will your product provide for them that they absolutely cannot live without?
- What is best way to convey this message to them?

- What will they respond to?
- What elements naturally draw them in? Audio? Video? Images?
- What is going to make them click a link?
- How should you introduce your product to your customer? What should your copy say on the first page they see?
- What is going to convince them to provide you with their email address?
- What is going to convince them to purchase your product?

To help understand what motivates your ideal customer, think about the following questions:

- What keeps your customers awake at night?
- What are they afraid of?
- What are they angry about?
- What are their top three daily frustrations?
- What do they desire most?
- Is there a built-in bias to the way they make decisions? (example: engineers are exceptionally analytical)
- Do they have their own jargon?
- Who else has tried to sell them something similar? How have they failed or succeeded?

Calls to Action

The final aspect we're going to look at is calls to action.

In a successful sales website, every page has a single, primary call to action. That is, an action you want your user to take.

Think of your sales website as a tunnel (or a funnel) you are trying to move your visitors through. Initially you want them to provide their email address. Any page they land on should include a prominent call to enter their email address, and perhaps a secondary call to purchase your product (or learn more about it).

For example, your home page should not be the standard collection of links, text and announcements that make them want to click in every direction.

A decent example of a home page with a call to action is DotNetInvoice.com (see screenshot above). The goal is to capture emails as people try our online demo.

A good example of a well-focused home page is BuildIT Systems[48]. This website (shown above) includes a large free trial button on the left, a bit of information about the product in the video, and a large call to action to get you to watch that video. This is a textbook example of putting your primary objective, which is to get someone to watch the video, front and center on the home page.

BlogJet[49] (see screenshot on the next page) is the final example. Personally, I would prefer a video in place of the screen shot, but their intent is not subtle: they want you to download their trial or buy the product. Any other action is completely out of your line of site.

If you want more information you can scroll down and see the video demo and testimonials. This is an impressive design that displays all the information you need for a purchase decision

---

[48] www.builditsystems.com

[49] www.codingrobots.com/blogjet/

on a single page, yet you don't feel overwhelmed with information. The elegance of this single page presentation cannot be understated, and they didn't arrive at it by accident.

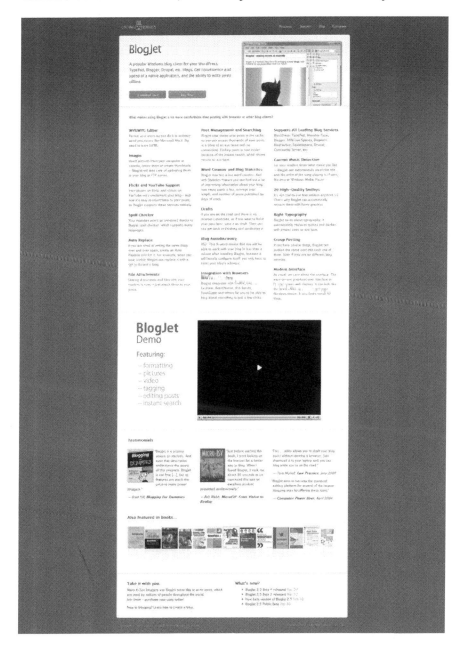

Seven Rules of Sales Site Design

Rule #1: The home page will not necessarily be the most visited page on your website. Search engines and deep linking [50]have changed this.

Rule #2: As a result of rule #1, every page needs a call to action. A visitor may first interact with your website through your Tour, Testimonials, or Pricing page. All of them should urge the user to take an action that gets them closer to providing you with their email, trying your demo, or making a purchase. Look at the bottom of every sub-page at DotNetInvoice.com for an example.

Rule #3: Every page needs a single focus. Think ruthlessly about eliminating extraneous functionality and duplicate information from your website. Each page should serve a single purpose and contain nothing to distract the user from that purpose.

Rule #4: Everything should be within 2 clicks. From any page, a visitor should be able to demo your product, buy your product, or provide you with their email address with two clicks, including the click of the "submit" button. This makes for a small and tight website with a single focus. For larger companies or sites which offer multiple products, this might not hold 100% true in every case.

Rule #5: Accommodate different reading patterns. Use headlines and bulleted lists for skimmers. Keep paragraphs unnaturally short for those who read every word.

Rule #6: Make buttons look like buttons. Make your buttons so clickable that people can't help but click them.

---

[50] Deep linking is the act of linking to internal pages on a website. Surprisingly, this was not common practice for the first several years of the internet's existence.

Rule #7: No One Reads. Text is a terrible selling tool; audio, video and images are always better.

The Pages

While it's impossible to provide a list of pages to include in your website for every potential startup idea, the vast majority of downloadable products and SaaS applications will perform well with five core pages.

The Core Pages

- Home
- Tour
- Testimonials
- Contact Us
- Pricing & Purchase

Home

The #1 goal of your home page is to convince your visitors to click 1 link. That's all you have to do to convince them not to leave is click a single link.

The key metric with home pages is abandonment rate (the number of people who leave without clicking a link). The book *Web Design for ROI* estimates that home pages have a 40-60% abandonment rate on average before they are optimized. This means that around half of all home page visitors leave without clicking a single link.

The solution? A simple home page with very few options, and large, clickable buttons.

Most websites don't implement this, but the ones that do have very high click through rates. Here are some examples you should strive to emulate:

Revive Africa (www.reviveafrica.com)

PopCap Games (www.popcap.com)

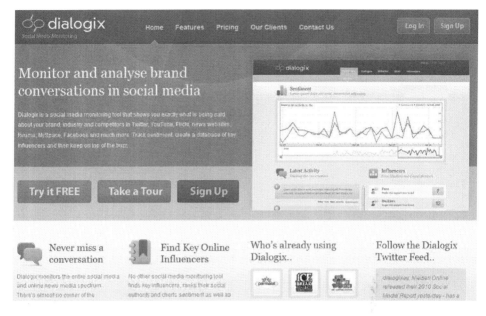

Dialogix (www.dialogix.com.au)

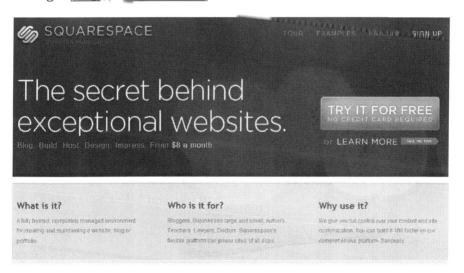

Squarespace (www.squarespace.com)

If you choose to have an image for your home page, choose one that shows the result of your product. For example, a home loan website should show people living in a house; a backpacking website should show people on top of a mountain, and an online proposal tool should show an image of a completed proposal.

Finding Your Hook

One of the most difficult pieces of marketing to create is your *hook*. Your hook is your four-second sales pitch and it should be the headline of your home page. It's the single sentence that grabs the reader in and makes her know she's in the right place.

- **DotNetInvoice's** hook is "Save Time. Get Paid Faster."
- **FogBugz's** hook is "Bring Your Project into Focus"
- **Basecamp's** hook is "The Better Way to Get Projects Done"
- **Bidsketch's** hook is "Simple Proposal Software Made for Designers"
- When it launched, the **iPod's** hook was "One Thousand Songs in Your Pocket"

These are 5-7 word summaries of your product. Each one conveys an image in your mind. Each one describes what the product does and (in most cases) who it's made for.

To find your hook you can take one of three approaches:

1. Explain what your product does and for whom. Such as "Simple proposal software made for designers."
2. Make a promise to the customer espousing a benefit of your product, such as "Save Time. Get Paid Faster."
3. Describe the single most remarkable feature of your product, such as "One Thousand Songs in Your Pocket."

Some other fake examples for something as boring as inventory software made for grocery stores:

1. **What it does and for whom:** Inventory Tracking for Grocery Stores
2. **Promise:** Automate Your Inventory
3. **Feature:** A Million Items at your Fingertips

Spend a few minutes brainstorming your hook and discuss it with a friend or colleague in your target market. Typically one of your choices will be obviously better than the others.

Once you've decided on a hook, you should put it as the header on your home page, and consider using it as your tagline. This hook is what will allow you to tell someone in 3 seconds what your product does, or at least why it's so cool that they need to check it out.

Tour Page

My recommendation for your tour page is to include medium-sized screen shots of the major screens filled with data, along with a one-minute screencast (video demo) of each page.

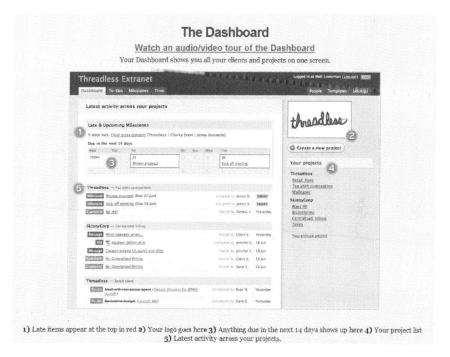

1) Late items appear at the top in red 2) Your logo goes here 3) Anything due in the next 14 days shows up here 4) Your project list 5) Latest activity across your projects.

This idea is shown on Basecamp's Tour page[51] (shown above), but I would opt for the screen shots to be smaller with the

---

[51] basecamphq.com/tour

ability to zoom in using the Highslide JS library[52], and include a clickable image of the video. People are much more likely to watch videos if they are presented visually as opposed to a "Watch this Video" text link.

Do your best to avoid large amounts of text on this page aside from the screen names and a 1-2 sentence description of each screen shot.

Testimonials

This page can also be titled "Buzz" or "Who uses [Your AppName]?" and it's one of the most important pages on your site. Do not launch without testimonials.

You will have beta testers, friends and colleagues who try your software – get a handful of testimonials and create this page.

Monitor mentions of your product using Google Alerts and add choice quotes and backlinks to this page. This not only adds to your list of buzz, but shows people that you will link to them if they write about your product.

Include any relevant logos to break up the page – otherwise it will be a boring page of text[53].

Needless to say, people won't read all of your testimonials so put your most important ones at the top.

Contact Us

It's best to provide both a contact form in the browser and a separate email address.

---

[52] www.highslide.com

[53] See http://www.dotnetinvoice.com/asp-net-web-host-billing-testimonials.aspx for an example of how to keep things interesting

In addition, always provide a toll-free number, even if you let it go to voice mail and return the calls. Many customers are turned away when they see you don't provide a phone number.

Also, including a physical address will inspire confidence for some visitors. I've found now that DotNetInvoice has a lot of testimonials and has been around for a few years people don't ask anymore, but at one point it was a big deal that I didn't provide a physical address on the site. I usually include only my city and state since I don't have an office and don't want to give out my home address.

However, there is a great service called *Earth Class Mail*[54] that allows you to pay around $20/month for a P.O. Box in a number of major U.S. cities (including New York, L.A., San Francisco, Seattle and Portland). You can also pay extra and get a physical address, but a P.O. Box works fine.

When you receive mail at this address they scan the first page and you receive an email notification. You can visit their site and tell them to shred it, forward it, or archive it. It's a cool system and one I wish I had signed up for before I decided to move 9 times in the last 10 years.

Pricing & Purchase
For SaaS applications this would be *Pricing & Sign-up*.

Unless you have a good reason to do otherwise, put this as the link on the far right of your top navigation and add subtle highlighting either by bolding the text or changing the color.

---

[54] www.earthclassmail.com

One of the best examples of a well-designed Pricing and Purchase page is at basecamphq.com/signup (see screenshot above).

A few things to notice that you should include on your own pricing page:

- No small text on this page – no paragraphs of description. Only large fonts.
- A call out to a 30-day free trial in large text.
- The pricing plans are shown with minimal description and in large fonts.
- One plan is highlighted as the best deal. It really makes you want to click it.
- Logos are shown just below the offerings
- There are a handful of frequently asked questions at the bottom (below where this screen shot cuts off) relating to payment and long-term contracts.
- At the bottom, there's a chance to ask any questions before you sign up

There are two other items I would include on your pricing page:

- If at all possible, include an Upsell. If you have add-on modules or services offer them here. If you have nothing else, allow customers to buy an extra year of support at a discount, or purchase priority support for an additional cost.
- If you don't offer a free trial, then at least offer a 30-day, no questions asked, money back guarantee. It may sound like crazy talk to do this with something like software, but the number of people who try to rip you off will pale in comparison to the number of people who purchase the product because of this guarantee. I've had a money back guarantee at DotNetInvoice for years and I've never regretted it.

Free Website Reviews

Once you've built your sales website, stop by Startup Lens[55] for a free five-minute screencast review of your site by yours truly. Click "submit your site" and it will be submitted into a queue that I pull from each week.

I will evaluate your site on how well you fit the above criteria.

While you're there, take a look at the previous reviews for pitfalls you can avoid with your sales website.

The Number One Goal of Your Website

Even in 2010, email is the most ubiquitous form of online communication. A 2007 study by E-mail Data Source indicated that 88% of U.S. adults had personal email accounts. And that was three years ago. If this percentage holds today, that means around 220 million U.S. adults have a personal email account.

Email is the most pervasive online communication tool, even over "hot" topics of yesterday and today such as blogs, RSS, Twitter and Facebook.

---

[55] www.startuplens.com

While each of these technologies has a place in your marketing arsenal, email has real potential to create substantial long-term value as you build your list over time.

"Email Marketing": A Four Letter Word

Your first thought when I say *email marketing* is probably "spam." But there's a huge difference between a spammer and what you will do when marketing your product via email.

First, you will never email someone without their permission. You will only send relevant emails to a small group of people who signed up to receive them specifically from you.

Second, every email you send will include an unsubscribe link so your recipients can unsubscribe at any time.

Lastly, you will never sell or rent out your email list. To do so would destroy the trust of your list.

Handle your subscribers with kid gloves and you'll be lauded for the information you provide to them. Abuse them and you will hear about it.

I've been on Joel Spolsky's mailing list since 2001. I've never once regretted the emails I receive from him, and if I did I could unsubscribe at any time. According to a comment he made on the Stack Overflow podcast[56], Joel's mailing list is in the mid to high five-figures. When he wants people to know about something he can get the word out quickly.

Don't let other peoples' abuse of email scare you away from an otherwise viable marketing channel.

Your Best Day Ever

One of my earlier successes with email lists was over two years ago. I had cobbled together a list of about 80 people interested in hearing about the next release of DotNetInvoice. I didn't

---

[56] blog.stackoverflow.com/category/podcasts/

know much about email marketing so it took about a year of answering sales questions and asking people one-on-one if they wanted to be added to the mailing list.

When the new version hit the street a hush fell over the internet. Copies were not flying off the shelves. I was pretty disappointed after all the time my business partner and I had invested.

So I decided to email our list of prospects. And sure enough, we sold five copies in a day.

Granted, this only amounted to $1,500, but the realization that my conversion rate was high (6%) and that having a list of 500 people of the same quality would result in a huge month for us, convinced me to invest more effort in gathering relevant emails from our healthy stream of traffic. I was leaving money (and satisfied customers) on the table every month by only collecting 7 or 8 emails.

Since then we have substantially increased our list and each new release beings a rush of sales once our list is notified. Each time we prepare for our new best day ever.

What would our sales be in a release month if we had a list the size of Joel Spolsky's? Now you know how he can afford those plush offices.

Building Your List
If you hang around someone who has successfully connected with an audience through email, you'll hear the phrase "building your list." This is the cornerstone of any successful email marketing activity – growing your email list with targeted, double opt-in email subscribers.

Targeted means the subscribers are interested in the laser-focused niche you've chosen.

Double opt-in means that after they enter their email address in your sign-up form, they will receive a confirmation link via email. Until they click on that link they are not added to your list. This ensures that your list is of the highest quality.

Let's take a look at the two list-building strategies you're likely to have success with:

Give Something Away

Have you ever seen the credit card tutorial PDF given away by Freckle Time Tracking[57]? Look at that PDF – it's awesome; the perfect example of providing an enormous amount of value for free.

If you're wondering why they gave it away, visit jumpstartcc.com. They got my email address and thousands more. The funny part is they don't even require you to give your email to download it. I gave them mine just because I want to see what they'll do next.

If your application helps designers track time, create a free report or whitepaper on How to Increase Your Hourly Rate by 50% Without Losing Business. With a few hours of research and interviews, you should be able to write a report on this subject. With a title like that and prominent placement of your sign-up form on your home page, you will receive email addresses.

If you sell beach towels, offer a free report on the Top 10 Expert Tips for Saving Money on your Beach Trip (an actual report I gave away on JustBeachTowels.com).

I recommend shooting for a PDF report from 5-15 pages.

The key is finding a topic that your audience will not only be interested in, but will be ravenous for. Once you have the title,

---

[57] http://www.scribd.com/doc/11037739/Jumpstart-credit-card-processing-version-1

you can create this work yourself or hire a writer to handle the leg work. I've had good luck finding writers on Elance.com.

Offer an Email Course

It sounds a bit hokey, but offering a free, five-day email course can be an exceptional draw. In general, more technical or web-savvy audiences prefer a longer report or white paper, while more non-technical users prefer email courses. But there's not a definitive line here, and the key is to test:

1. First create your report and offer it as a PDF download for one-month. Note the number of sign-ups you receive.
2. Next, break the report up into a five-day email course and offer it for one month. Compare results and go with what works.

I've offered an email course on *Becoming a Programmer* that's been wildly successful in building a relationship with an audience I would otherwise have had a single contact point and then would have been out of their minds forever.

Nuts and Bolts

Hopefully by now, you're on board with the idea of building your mailing list. So what's next?

The first step is to get email list management software in place: you need a form on your website to collect emails, somewhere to store them, the ability to add unsubscribe links to the bottom of your emails, run spam assassin on outgoing emails to ensure they won't get caught in spam filters, send both HTML and text emails, track clicks and other metrics, send sequential emails when someone signs up, guard against being blacklisted by people clicking "spam" in their mail client...and on and on...

Needless to say, you won't be building a list management system yourself, *nor will you be hosting it yourself.* This is the #1 mistake I've seen software entrepreneurs make with regards to list management; trying to host the software themselves.

Aside from the hassles of maintenance, email deliverability should be your #1 priority, and you will never achieve the level of deliverability that third party services achieve.

The hoops they go through and the amount of communication between mailing list providers and ISPs is astounding. They have full-time staff dedicated to sorting out blacklisting problems, spam complaints, and increasing deliverability. You will never come close to achieving their level of deliverability and given how hard you work to gather every email address, it is absolutely worth ensuring they all arrive at their destination.

Provider

I've managed several mailing lists over the years and the one provider I recommend is MailChimp[58].

MailChimp is a relatively young service (founded in 2004), and combines gorgeous design and usability with three pricing models: a free plan, a per-email pricing model of about $.03 per email, or a flat monthly fee ($10/month for 500 subscribers, $30/month for 2,500).

They also have amazing email templates. MailChimp is a great place to get started since you can build your list slowly and pay as you go. MailChimp offers a solid platform for getting started and should provide for your needs for quite some time.

What to Send

There are two types of mailing lists:

Relevant Information

If you target a niche with a common interest, such as personal trainers or psychologists, providing ongoing content every 2-4 weeks is the best way to build a relationship. Think of your mailing list as a blog with a new post every 2-4 weeks (to gain

---

[58] www.mailchimp.com

SEO benefit from your newsletter content, you should also post it to your blog).

A powerful tip I've used extensively is to use an autoresponder series, which is a series of emails sent in a specific order to new subscribers with pre-determined gaps between each email. With an autoresponder series you can write content once and have it be re-used for years.

As long as you don't cover topics dealing with current events, you should start your mailing list not by sending broadcast emails every 2-4 weeks, but by building your autoresponder series with a 2-4 week gap between each email.

Then, the first person who signs up will receive the first email, then a two week gap, then the second email. And the 500th person who signs up a year down the line will receive the same first email, a two week gap, and the same second email. In this manner none of your content is wasted; you haven't created throw-away emails early in your list, every email you write will be used numerous times as new people join your list.

When you need to send time-sensitive information, such as a product launch announcement, simply send a one-time broadcast to your list. Your email autoresponder series won't be impacted.

You can always go back and edit or delete emails in your series if they become out of date.

Product Updates
This is the type of list we run at DotNetInvoice. The problem we've run into is finding ongoing information relevant to all of our customers, since they are small business people in a variety of industries.

With DotNetInvoice, the only thing our prospects have in common is they are interested in an invoicing solution, which is a horizontal market. There's very little interesting content to be created on that subject. This is why we've elected to use our email list to provide product launch updates and to ask for peoples' opinions on the future direction. Even with this lower level of involvement and a lot fewer emails being sent, you'd be surprised at the response rates.

Content

A question that always arises is: what kind of information should I send to my list?

The key is to **be relevant**. Maintaining high relevance is critical to keeping people subscribed.

Idea #1: Monitor Current Events

If you have the option to go with an information list instead of simply product updates, the next step is to monitor the following news sources and report to your audience on new happenings in their niche:

- Google Alerts
- Digg
- YouTube
- The popular blogs in this niche

Take this information and share relevant links with a small amount of commentary. These are the best kinds of posts – easy to write but containing a lot of value for your audience. Most audiences (software developers and web designers excluded) are out of touch with current events in their industry so it's dead simple to provide relevant content with a few minutes of time every few weeks.

Idea #2: Q&A

Another great source of content is questions from customers or prospects. Answer the question in your email to solidify your place as an expert in this niche.

Idea #3: Interviews

Short email interviews with a current customer on how they use your software are always interesting. You could also leverage a well known blogger in the industry. These shouldn't take more than 30-45 minutes to put together since all you're doing is sending a list of questions to someone (once you have their permission) and publishing them in your email. In exchange, the customer/blogger gets exposure for himself.

Idea #4: Hire a Writer

Hire a writer from Elance[59] and have them write an original short-form article on a subject of your choosing. It will cost $20-30, but if it contains unique information, it can make your subscribers happy, and may also get your email forwarded, which will grow your list.

Strategies for Sending Emails

Here are seven critical tips for improving deliverability and getting people to open your emails.

1. **Time of Day/Week** – It isn't apparent at first glance, but the time of day and day of the week you send your email will have a major impact on how many people open it. The real answer to "when should I send?" is to test for yourself by splitting your list and sending the same email at different times. But as a general rule, Tuesdays, Wednesdays and Thursdays are the best days, between 7am and 10:30am.

2. **HTML vs. Plain Text** – The answer is: you should always send at least plain text, since many mobile devices don't read HTML emails. So the real question is: should you bother with HTML? It depends. If your audience is designers, marketers, or people otherwise interested in attractive packages then you should. If you're dealing with technical types or lay-people, you

---

[59] www.elance.com

can very likely get away with text emails. Both of the providers mentioned above provide HTML email templates so you can segment your list and try both options to see which converts for your audience.

3. **Never Send Attachments** – They hurt deliverability and many will be stripped by spam filters. Upload the file to a server and send a link instead.

4. **Pay Attention to Your "From" Name & Address** – Look at an email in your email client – notice how the "from" address reads. It's surprising how many emails I receive with "Admin" in the "from" name. At least put "[ProductName] Support" or "[ProductName] Newsletter" to provide some indication of who you are. And if you have a more personal relationship with your audience feel free to put your real name.

5. **Your Subject is Your Headline** - Perhaps the only factor that determines if your mail gets opened is your subject line. You must hone and craft your ability to write engaging subject lines in 7 words or less. Here are some guidelines:

    a. **The shorter the better.**

    b. **Ask a question** in your subject and answer it in the emails. Example: *A DotNetInvoice Super-Bowl Ad?*

    c. **Make a partial statement** with "…" at the end and continue the sentence in your email. Example: *A Free Copy of DotNetInvoice Every Day…*

    d. **Use the recipient's first name** in the subject line. Example: *Rob, DotNetInvoice is Free for 24 hours…*

    e. **Include your product's #1 benefit** in the subject. Example: *Save 5 Hours of Time This Month*

    f. **Don't exaggerate.** Deliver on anything your subject promises.

    g. **Avoid spam filters** by watching your spam score. MailChimp will parse your subject and body and tell you if your email looks spammy. This is most often caused by using words like: free, money back guarantee, click here, and using all caps in the subject. See this article[60] from MailChimp on some other (common sense) things to avoid.

6. **Have One Goal for Each Email** – Is this a relationship-building email filled with information, or do you have a call to action for it? If you have a call to action, make it prominent and ask people to act. As a rule of thumb, every fourth or fifth email can contain a more sales-y message.

7. **Test, Test, Test** – It's all about finding out your audience's preferences. Both email services I recommend have the ability to segment your audience while sending broadcasts. Test the time of day, day of week and subjects. It will be obvious fairly quickly which approach is superior.

The Ideal Launch

To finish this chapter, I'd like to briefly discuss a concept I call *The Ideal Launch.*

Several months ago, a startup founder asked me for my description of the ideal startup launch. It's a simple vision, and it looks something like this:

Step 1: Six Months Before Launch

Six months before your launch date, use your audience on Twitter, Facebook and your blog to send traffic to your startup's home page. The home page gives a brief description of your product and offers them a deal if they provide their email address to be notified of the launch.

---

[60] http://www.mailchimp.com/blog/most-common-spam-filter-triggers/

Step 2: Over the Next Six Months

Over the next six months create buzz around your product by guest blogging, sending interesting updates to your social networks, commenting on blogs and forums and generally engaging your target audience, always sending them to your home page.

Step 4: One Week Before Launch

Approximately one week before launch (preferably on a Tuesday, Wednesday or Thursday), email your list of targeted email addresses. Let them know that your product will be launching next week and that since they are on your mailing list, they will receive a special price available only to those on the list, but that the price will only last for 48 hours.

Tell them the day and time they will receive the email.

Step 4: Launch Day

On launch day, email your list. Almost immediately, sales will start rolling in. You're going to have the best sales day you will see for a while.

Conversion rates on targeted mailings can be 20%+. A few hundred sales of your $19/month SaaS application is not a bad way to kick-start your startup.

Step 5: Thirty Six Hours After Launch

Send your list a final email informing them that the deal will end in 12 hours. You will receive another few sales before you close down your special pricing.

There are more complex variations to this, but it's a simple, proven approach to increasing your launch-day sales by ten-fold. Without some variation of the above, you will be lucky to sell 10 licenses in your first week.

Chapter 5

Startup Marketing

Don't Believe Everything You Read About Startup Marketing

Judging by the blogs, books, podcasts and conferences of today, it seems like you can base the marketing for an entire company on a Facebook page and a Twitter account.

The reality is, although these social avenues are new, fun and exciting, they have not replaced the fundamental internet marketing approaches that were themselves the new, fun and exciting approaches of five years ago.

We want to believe that these new tools are the best way to market a startup, because it's fun, social and public. But except for rare exceptions, the return on investment is dubious at best.

Core strategies like building an audience, search engine optimization and participating in niche communities have far more impact on your bottom line than most of the new media tools you read about in the business press.

To begin this chapter, realize that everything you've heard about marketing on Twitter and Facebook is true, but with a few minor details left out. Such as the fact that the companies who have used Twitter to turn a profit have tens of thousands of subscribers which they've built up over hundreds and hundreds of hours of effort over the past few years.

The same applies to Facebook. None of this is a shortcut. Nothing happens overnight.

So while setting up a Twitter account is a fine strategy, realize that it will take months to build any kind of following, and it is extremely unlikely that Twitter will ever be one of your main sales channels.

While there is value to Twitter in terms of customer service and being active in the online community, this chapter is going to focus on tactics that will drive targeted prospects to your website that have the potential to result in sales.

With that introduction, let's take a look at the goals you're trying to achieve as you market your startup.

Marketing is Not One Size Fits All

If you take away nothing else from this chapter, know this:

> *Many approaches will not work in your market.*

For example: using Twitter to market to pool cleaners is not going to yield great results. Targeting web designers in the same way could be wildly successful.

This is so important that I want to say it one more time: only certain marketing tactics will benefit your startup. *Those tactics will change, depending on the niche you're in.*

This means that when you read about a new social media marketing approach, you must understand your market well enough to have an idea if that approach will work or not.

Much like building a good software application requires an understanding of your users, gaining an understanding of your marketing is your first step to building a successful business.

The Importance of Traffic Quality

Traffic quality plays a huge role in how well your website converts visitors into customers.

By *quality,* I mean the following: how close each visitor is to your ideal customer and how much of a relationship you have with that visitor.

> *High quality traffic means each visitor is very close to your ideal customer and they know and trust you.*

This is why TechCrunch traffic is not profitable for startups. Unless your niche market is other startups, it's completely untargeted traffic and you have no relationship with the audience. Using our definition above, this traffic is of low quality.

Traffic quality also becomes apparent the first time you send an email to a list that you've been communicating with for some length of time. Your conversion rate for these visitors will be astronomically higher than your standard website traffic; as much as 10x higher in fact. This is because the quality is so much better.

This is important because it means you can focus your energy on driving high quality sources of traffic.

If people from your email list convert at 5-10x the rate of someone finding your site through Google, you can spend 5-10x the effort getting people on your mailing list and still have a break-even ROI.

Likewise, if you see the massive amount of traffic from organic search, you have to know how many of those people are buying your product. Without that knowledge you are flying blind and cannot properly allocate your time.

Luckily, Google Analytics[61] can spell this out for you using goals[62].

After doing this, you will begin to see that many sources of traffic do not convert *at all*. And you can stop pursuing that traffic and focus your efforts on methods that bring in sales.

While it's nice to have several thousand people visit your website, if they don't convert, they may as well have not shown up at all. Don't think you're building a brand – you're not Coca-Cola or Johnson & Johnson. The minute those users leave your site you are out of their minds forever.

The Two Tiers of Traffic

It's impossible to say which source of traffic is best for every website, but having launched or revamped over 20 revenue-generating websites and worked with hundreds of software entrepreneurs, there is a definite pattern to which traffic strategies can sustain a business, and which serve as supplemental.

Top Shelf: Traffic Strategies that Will Sustain a Business
1. A Mailing List
2. A Blog, Podcast or Video Blog
3. Organic Search

Second Shelf: Supplemental Traffic Strategies
1. Social Media / Social Networks
2. Pay-per-click Advertising

---

[61] http://www.google.com/analytics/

[62] For more info on setting up goals, visit http://tinyurl.com/69yw2b

3. Forums
4. Press Releases
5. Guest Blogging
6. Affiliate Programs
7. Banner and other advertising
8. Everything else...

The first thing you might be thinking is "But I've heard of someone who made a boatload of money using Twitter."

This *might* be true, but one of three things is likely:

1. It didn't really happen, but it makes a good story.
2. The person did not build a sustainable business. We're looking for a long-term approach that we can build a business on.
3. This person was not selling a software/web/mobile application made for a niche audience.

Due to the infinite and ever-growing number of Second Shelf traffic strategies, we're not going to cover them in this book. In addition, many Second Shelf strategies are highly time-intensive for the return they provide, and they vary widely from market to market. This means that many won't apply in your particular niche.

The Point

The point is to understand that investing time in Twitter[63] and Facebook[64] is a fun diversion and can bring traffic or notoriety to your business, but the way to build long-term, sustainable traffic that will sustain a real business is through Top Shelf traffic strategies.

---

[63] twitter.com

[64] www.facebook.com

Building an audience through a mailing list, blog or podcast is by far the best source of traffic. I encourage you to try at least one.

And finally, search engine optimization (SEO) is a must. At a minimum you should create a keyword list and perform on-page SEO, with your next steps focusing on link building strategies to raise your organic search rankings.

A Word about Pay-per-click Advertising

Although some build entire businesses on pay-per-click (PPC) advertising, it's not something I recommend as a long-term approach.

My recommendation for PPC is to use it for finding keywords that convert for you, and spend the time and money to search engine optimize for those terms. Pouring a never-ending supply of money into Google AdWords is no way to build a business.

The benefit of PPC (in particular Google AdWords) is they are easy to get started, fast to turn off, and you can make adjustments in near real-time. This flexibility comes at a price, which is pretty sure to rise over time.

So instead of looking at PPC as a long-term marketing approach, use it as a shortcut for finding keywords that convert and work on ranking organically for those terms.

A Closer Look at Top Shelf Traffic Strategies

Now that we've defined the Top Shelf traffic strategies, we're going to spend the rest of this chapter examining some guidelines for implementing each.

Each of these topics has had numerous books written on the subject. Given the scope of these topics, we won't be able to cover them in step-by-step detail, but I will look at how you should approach them and recommend further reading if needed.

Strategy #1: A Mailing List

A mailing list is the most effective marketing tool you will possess. It works in any market. It's a marketing *requirement* for startups.

As discussed in chapter 4, building a mailing list is not only pivotal to The Ideal Launch plan, but it should be the #1 goal of your website. Getting people to engage with you, to listen to and trust you will have more impact on sales than any other marketing approach.

Over time, your list will become an incredible asset. If you treat your list right, offering insight, discounts, perks and useful information, over time it will become invaluable to your business.

The best day revenue your startup ever has will be the day you cash in a bit of your list equity and email them with a time-limited promotion. You will be shocked at the number of sales you can make in 6 hours.

We covered mailing lists in chapter 4 so we won't cover them again here.

Strategy #2: A Blog, Podcast or Video Blog

Blogs, podcasts and video blogs require a certain amount of unique insight or expertise. If you don't have this, partner with someone who does. For every person like yourself looking to gain the audience of a market so you can promote your software, there is someone with insider knowledge looking to be recognized as an expert in that same market.

Realistically, the choice of blog, podcast or video blog depends on your skill with the written/spoken word, and the kind of content your market niche consumes. The latter is far more important than the former.

My recommendation is to start with either blogging or podcasting until you've built an audience. You'll find there is so much to learn about creating content that trying to do so in multiple formats will require too much of an up-front time investment.

Branching into the other approaches is a good way to expand your reach, but is too much to bite off on your first day. For now, let's look in detail at the benefits of each approach.

Blogging

A blog is second to a mailing list in most markets because blog readers tend to be more passive. Mailing lists come into your inbox where you must read or delete, whereas blog subscribers are much more likely to hit "mark as read" on a list of blogs.

However, in technical markets, you'll be hard-pressed to build a mailing list of developers. Developers tend to stay away from things that clog their inbox, typically opting for RSS feeds instead.

But do not be fooled; for the rest of the world email is by far the better way to communicate with your audience.

With that said, blogs offer twice the marketing punch by catering to both your audience and the search engines.

Audience #1: People

If you spend a year or two writing engaging, original posts, submitting them to social media sites, and prominently displaying your RSS and email subscription icons, you will gradually build an audience of readers who learn to know and trust you.

This impact, while less than a mailing list of the same people, is invaluable. The trust they develop for you and the relationship you're able to build over time is worth many times more than a new website visitor.

Audience #2: Search Engines

In addition to writing for your audience, you should also optimize your blog for search engines, tweak your posts to target specific search keywords, and let Google drive traffic to your blog.

Visitors who come across your blog via search engines are new and won't have the trust level of regular readers, but they are also a constant stream of free, incoming traffic.

Even if the conversion rates are low, a few hundred (or a few thousand) people seeing your content for the first time every month is a solid asset.

Does a blog have some kind of SEO advantage over a standard website? Yes and no.

A blog doesn't have an advantage just because it uses a blogging engine. Google doesn't care that instead of static HTML you're using WordPress, or that instead of a brochure website you have posts published in reverse chronological order.

A 10-page static sales website and a 10-page WordPress blog with content that never changes look virtually the same in the eyes of Google.

However, blogs are not 10-page, static websites (whereas most sales sites are). Blogs have several advantages that play right into what Google wants:

1. Google views a website with constantly updating content as alive and relevant, and it will rank higher. Blogs are made precisely for this purpose.
2. Google likes large quantities of content and blogs tend toward that direction over time.
3. Google likes individual pages that focus on a theme. Blogs are ideal for this since every new post is its own page.

4. Google likes straightforward link structures such as the fact that nearly every blog has an archive page that links to every post ever published, and category pages that group posts into categories (called silos in SEO-speak).

Indeed, blogs are light years ahead of static sales websites in terms of drawing search engine credibility.

Can You Blog for Both?

This is not a mutually exclusive situation. You don't have to focus on one or the other; it actually helps to focus on both an audience and search engines. If you enjoy the interaction with an audience, the long-term benefits of a community of people who trust you are undeniable.

But at the same time, blogging for an audience is not for everyone. It's time consuming and requires a steady stream of unique, well-written posts.

Blogging for search engines doesn't mean you can post garbage content, but it does lift the burden of having to be truly original all the time.

Writing basic posts focused on keywords and building no audience whatsoever can still be an absurdly valuable asset to your business and is much easier than trying to build a real blog audience.

Does Every Product Need a Blog?

Most products you launch should have their own blog, if for nothing else than to draw search engine traffic. This is especially true if you're in a non-competitive search market, where having a 2-year old blog with a few incoming links allows you to rank #1 for your keywords.

Podcasting and Video Blogging

After several years in existence, podcasting and video blogging are still fluid mediums. While the worldwide podcasting and video blog watching audiences are small compared to blogs and infinitesimal compares to mailing lists, the engagement achieved from talking to your listeners is unprecedented. Blogs and mailing lists can't touch it.

While the overall audience is smaller for these media, the competition in most niches is also weak or non-existent. And the bond you are able to build with an audio or video audience is unachievable with the written word. There's absolutely no comparison.

The hurdle with podcasting and video blogging is that they aren't consumed by most markets. They are time intensive to produce, and they require a certain level of talent to create episodes that keep people interested.

With that said, if you're working in an area where you are an expert, you should be able to turn out a 30-minute podcast in under 90 minutes of prep and recording time, plus 2-3 hours of editing, which you should outsource

For video, it depends on your format. If you're into raw, unedited content like Gary Vaynerchuk's Wine Library[65] you can crank out a 15-minute video in... 15 minutes. If you opt for heavy editing and production value you can easily spend several hours on a 15-minute episode.

Obviously the details of starting a podcast or video blog are beyond the scope of this book. If you are thinking of starting a podcast, the book *Podcasting for Dummies*[66] is an excellent overview for getting started.

For video blogging, I recommend the book *Get Seen: Online Video Secrets to Building Your Business*[67].

---

[65] tv.winelibrary.com

[66] http://tinyurl.com/22q8l3q

[67] http://tinyurl.com/29t2ekc

Either one is worth the $20 to get a better idea of whether it's something you want to pursue.

Strategy #3: Organic Search

Harnessing organic search requires one thing: search engine optimization (SEO). SEO is the science of optimizing your website to improve its rankings in search engines.

Some argue that SEO is somehow "gaming the system" and pushing junk websites to the top of the rankings.

The true answer: it is. There are tons of junk sites at the top of search engines simply because they know how to play the game.

But there's an interesting line to walk. For example, Google provides a Search Engine Optimization Starter Guide[68] that discusses page titles, Meta tags, URL structure, and other basic SEO information that *helps Google understand what your website is about* as this improves their search results.

SEO *can* be about gaming the system, but it can also be about making sure your website is presented in an optimized form that search engines can clearly and readily understand.

To take an example: if you're a blogger you may have heard that you should use keywords with high search volume in your post titles. Some might look at this as gaming the system, but if you're providing content that's relevant to this term, don't you want to organize your posts around terms where people can find them?

It's actually more helpful to use commonly used terms in your post titles than to use confusing or low volume search terms. This could be considered gaming the system. I argue that it's making your post more relevant to your audience.

[68] http://www.google.com/webmasters/docs/search-engine-optimization-starter-guide.pdf

The Two Faces of SEO

There are an overwhelming number of resources available on SEO, and an overwhelming volume of information. The problem is that SEO is rarely broken down into its simplest forms. SEO is only two components: on-page factors and incoming links.

On-page factors include anything you have direct control over such as your page titles, Meta tags, URL structures, and even your domain name. We will not cover on-page factors here as they have been covered ad nauseam in every beginning SEO book and website in existence.

On-page factors are the simple part of SEO. Do not get caught up in the apparent complexity or mystery surrounding SEO. Implement your on-page SEO and move on.

If you need a reference for on-page SEO, I recommend the book *Search Engine Optimization an Hour a Day*[69].

Incoming links are the currency of the internet. A link implies trust and credibility. The more links you receive from relevant, authoritative websites, the more authority Google will grant your site.

Link building is the "hard" part of SEO. Links are a challenge to build, they take time or money, and the link economy of the web is complex.

However, there are a handful of link building guidelines that simplify this complex system into an understandable ecosystem. While the science of building links is as complex as Google's algorithm itself, these simplified rules bring to light the elements you should focus on when building links for your own website.

---

[69] http://tinyurl.com/27gr5p6

Link Building Guidelines

Guideline #1: Not All Links Are Created Equal

The ideal link for your website is a link from an aged website that itself has tons of incoming links. The ideal link would come from a page with a high PageRank and few outgoing links – the more outgoing links from a page, the more the PageRank is diluted. Finally, the website should be extremely relevant to the topic of your site.

On the other end of the spectrum, we have a new or un-trusted domain, a page with hundreds of outbound links, and a site that's totally unrelated to your topic.

The first kind of link can be worth orders of magnitude more than the second link.

Guideline #2: Vary Link Text

The search engines are smart these days. If you build a large number of links pointing to your home page in a short period of time, all using the link text "Invoicing Software," you're going to set off a red flag.

This is why you should optimize a page for multiple related keywords. Instead of just "Invoicing Software" you could also use "ASP.NET Invoicing Software," "Software for Invoicing" and "Invoice Program" (assuming your page is optimized for these terms).

My general rule is to focus 50% of your links on your most important term for that page, and the other 50% spread across the other 3-5 terms that page is targeting.

Guideline #3: Build Links Over Time

Did I mention search engines are smart? If you build 120 links in a month, or 10 links per month for a year, the second scenario is going to play out far more in your favor.

The engines know that authoritative websites receive constant, ongoing citations from around the web. Receiving a big chunk of links at once is only helpful if you continue to build links at a steady pace each month.

Guideline #4: Stay Out of Bad Neighborhoods

"Bad neighborhoods" are areas of the web that search engines look at with disdain. These are your link farms that consist mainly of free for all links (FFA) pages. Their links are worthless.

You can typically spot these sites by their spammy or non-existent content, myriad of links, and typically a large number of obnoxious ads. Never link to sites like this.

In addition, reciprocal links are dead and gone. Search engines wised up to them long ago. Anyone suggesting you exchange links with them, even using a "ring" approach where site 1 links to site 2, site 2 links to site 3 and on around until site 100 links back to site 1, have been long foiled by Google.

How to Build Links

Link building is the real work of SEO. There are several key approaches for building links that keep you in good neighborhoods, and will, over time allow you to raise your rank in the search engines.

Approach #1: Directories

Directories have lost a lot of impact as search engine algorithms have improved. But there are still directories worth submitting to.

The general directories where I submit my websites are:

- **DMOZ** (www.dmoz.org) – Free. Although its importance has diminished over the years, it's still worth submitting to. You only get one crack at it, so link to your home page and choose your link text carefully. A DMOZ listing can be worth 10-20 links from lower end directories.

- **JoeAnt** (www.joeant.com) – $40
- **Gimpsy** (www.gimpsy.com) – Free for a 6-month turnaround, and increasing in price to $49 for a 3-day turnaround.

I haven't found an automated submission package worth the $5 you'll pay for it. Save your time and money.

Approach #2: Niche & Local Directories

If you sell software relating to graphic designers, do a Google search for the following terms:

- graphic design software directory
- design software directory

Many directory submissions are free. Choose your link text wisely and submit to each one by hand.

Approach #3: Competitor Backlinks

Websites that link to your competition will more than likely have an interest in linking to you. Using Yahoo! Site Explorer[70], look at your competitors' backlinks and determine if it's appropriate to email the linking site's owner and ask for your site to be added to the list.

Approach #4: Google Alerts

Google alerts[71] is one of the most under-used tools in online marketing.

Create an alert for all variations of your product names, company names, competitors' names, and your name, as well as quoted terms with high relevance to your product. You'll want to make them highly relevant and quoted to avoid an overwhelming barrage of results every day.

---

[70] siteexplorer.search.yahoo.com

[71] www.google.com/alerts

If someone is talking about a problem that you can solve, make an intelligent comment or contribution and include a link to your product. You must be careful to walk the line of sounding non-commercial, especially when commenting on a blog.

Approach #5: Publishing Articles
Article marketing is an under-utilized startup marketing tool. Article marketing is a good way to get targeted links into the hands of article repositories, with the potential of having your article reprinted on websites and blogs that use syndicated content from these directories.

Note: the pages of the article repositories themselves don't typically rank in Google since the articles are re-printed all over the internet and Google doesn't give much credit these days for duplicate content.

Of the thousands of article repositories on the web you should consider three:

- **EzineArticles** (ezinearticles.com)
- **GoArticles** (www.goarticles.com)
- **iSnare** (www.isnare.com)

The key to article marketing is to submit unique, focused niche articles that link back to your website using specific link text to help your SEO (remember to choose keywords carefully, and to follow the article guidelines set up by the websites regarding the number and nature of the links you can place in each article).

You can write the articles yourself or, depending on the subject, hire someone to write them for you. There are thousands of article writers available on Elance, and I've received good results with keyword-focused articles from $3-$8 per article, depending on length.

Here are a few other recommendations:

- Most article sites have bio boxes. These are often the only area where you can use anchor text and links. Typically you would only place a brief bio with a link to your site, but if the bio box has no physical box around it on the page (as is the case with EzineArticles), include your last paragraph of text in your bio and add one additional anchor text link here. People are inclined to click on link in an article far more than in a bio box.
- iSnare costs $2 to submit to thousands of article repositories. While you don't get much benefit from being in thousands of repositories, the real benefit happens if your content is reprinted elsewhere on the web. At that point, contact the webmaster of that site and offer to write unique content for them. That will provide unique content and a backlink to you.
- For articles, 500-700 words is best. You need 500 to be over the minimum length requirements, and over 700 words most people won't read it.
- In your bio, include "http://" plus your URL in case your article is syndicated in plain text.

Approach #6: Offer a Free Academic/Non-profit Version of Your Product in Exchange for a Link

Do some good for the world and get a link out of it.

The best part is that academic and many non-profit organizations have authority status in Google because they are long-standing websites and don't link to many commercial sites. Their links can be easily worth many times that of a link from a typical website.

Approach #7: Testimonials

Contact companies whose products you use and offer to provide a testimonial if they will include a link to your website. When you send the testimonial, be specific about your link text, which should include your keywords if possible.

Approach #8: Buy Links

This will be the most controversial strategy discussed and is considered a questionable approach by some. Most of the webmasters I know buy and sell links.

There is a large link economy that flies under the radar of Google and the other search engines. Google will penalize or drop your website if they find out you are buying or selling links.

There are two main strategies for buying links:

1. **Link Rental.** The most prominent company for buying and selling links is **Text-link-ads.com** (TLA). They are so prominent that you cannot find them in Google, even if you search on the phrase "text link ads" (though you can find them when searching on "text-link-ads.com"). They offer reasonable pricing and an informative guide to link buying[72] I recommend you read if you're going to explore this route. The major drawback to TLA is they are a "link rental" service, meaning you pay a recurring monthly fee for your links. This gets expensive rather quickly.

2. **Buying Links.** The other option is to find services who will build permanent links for you. A Google search for "contextual link building" will unearth many such services. Expect to pay $5-$20 per link for permanent contextual links, depending on the page rank of the website.

Conclusion

By focusing on the Top Shelf marketing strategies and sprinkling in supplemental strategies aimed at your market, you can build an optimal, custom marketing approach for your

---

[72] http://www.text-link-ads.com/r/starter_kit

niche that will work far better than the "hot" new social media marketing approach you read about in the tech press.

Chapter 6

Virtual Assistants and Outsourcing

What is a Virtual Assistant?

A virtual assistant (VA) is a remote worker hired to complete tasks you prefer not to do, or should not be doing as the founder of a startup.

These can be research tasks, like finding every tech blogger who blogs about cats, repetitive tasks like creating 100 affiliate links for products in a Word document, or ongoing tasks like monitoring a handful of job boards and posting new jobs to your website.

The term VA has grown to describe any remote contract worker, including people who help with audio editing, video editing, bookkeeping, webmaster tasks, link building, and so on. A VA can be domestic or international, as long as they have a computer and an email account.

Why Should My Startup Use a Virtual Assistant?

Outsourcing to a virtual assistant will dramatically reduce the time you need to spend on administrative tasks, and increase the time you can commit to growing your business.

The value proposition of a VA deals with how you monetize your time. If you monetize your time at $50/hour and you can pay a VA $6/hour to handle administrative tasks, this frees up time for you to create real value in your business by developing new features or expanding marketing efforts.

Performing tasks you could pay someone else $6 to accomplish is a foolish use of an entrepreneur's time.

My VAs have saved me literally hundreds of hours over the past few years.

Case Study: How I Launched One Month Earlier Using Outsourcing

More than two years ago, my business partner and I discussed launching a hosted version of our invoicing software, DotNetInvoice.

We developed the plan and task list, and estimated the effort at around 160 hours including development time needed to make DotNetInvoice a multi-tenant application. But given the heavy competition in the hosted invoicing software market and the level of effort of the task, it was continually placed on the back burner.

The Shearing

After our initial 160 hour estimate, every six months or so for the past two years we've revisited the idea of a hosted version until one day in November of last year. On this day we came to the realization that we didn't need to make DotNetInvoice multi-tenant in order to have a hosted version. The other invoicing players are multi-tenant because they coded their invoicing services from scratch, but it's not the only way to do it.

The more we thought about it we realized the benefits to keeping it a single-tenant application: the ease of migrating from our hosted version to a downloaded version, and keeping each customer's data separated in its own database to name two.

The interesting thing is that once that large task was removed from the list, other things began to fall off, as well.

At this point we begin looking at the launch of Hosted DotNetInvoice as a market test; to see if we could build enough of a customer base to warrant a major investment in the hosted invoicing market space. With that in mind, things started flying off our "must-have" list.

The next largest piece was automating sign-up and provisioning of a new hosted installation. In an ideal world, when a customer wants a new hosted account they would fill out a web form with all of their information and their new hosted version would be ready in 30 seconds. But that amount of automation – given the fact that we have to create a new sub-domain, a new database, and copy physical files – would take a substantial amount of time to develop and QA. So we tossed it.

The final thing we threw out was the need for a custom purchase page; a page where someone enters their details to make the purchase. In a desperate attempt to bring this entire project down to less than two days work we simply utilized PayPal subscriptions. Not the optimal approach, but it works quite well for testing out an idea before we invest another day into this project.

Iteration vs. Automation

As a developer, the features I mentioned above seem like a necessity from day one. *Not* automating this process creates the ongoing repetitive work that computers are designed to handle. Manual work...this is what computers are supposed to save us from!

But by getting over the need to automate everything to infinite scale and putting a VA in charge of manually creating new hosted accounts, the time investment to get this feature launched dropped from 160 hours of work to about 10 hours.

I can hear the cries of developers around the world as I write this: "You can't launch a half-baked solution! You'll never go back and fix it!"

Most of us have worked in corporate environments where you're never allowed to go back and refactor code. This burns into our psyche that you don't want to launch a semi-functioning solution because you'll never have time to go back and fix it.

But the benefits of being my own boss and being a tiny software company are that I can come back to this anytime. In fact, the day the amount of money paid to my VA for handling this task exceeds a certain amount, I will be very motivated to automate it.

Ideally, by the time I code it up, we'll have many customers using the platform which means I'll be working on a product I know is viable, and that's paying for the time I'm spending to automate it.

Agile Development, meet Agile Business.

Through a bit of outsourcing to a VA, you can get to market with less up-front expense and in dramatically less time than if you try to automate everything.

Had we chosen to automate everything, the worst potential outcome would have been investing 160 hours of time (a *huge* amount of time for a startup), and then scrapping the whole thing. When you're working on a small team you can't afford to throw away that much time.

The Lesson
The lesson is that before you launch your product, what are some processes you can avoid automating? How about

reminder emails? How about monthly billing? Could a human being run a report once a month and send emails or charge credit cards?

This is not the paradigm we typically think of as developers because we're used to enterprise IT shops where everything has to scale infinitely.

As a startup, you'll have plenty of time before you need to scale, and you may never need to scale if the idea doesn't work. Every hour spent writing code is wasted time if that code could be replaced by a human being doing the same task until your product proves itself.

The Two Points When a VA is Most Helpful

There are two key points during the life of your startup where your life will be much easier if you use a virtual assistant (VA):

1. While proving out your product
2. After your product launch

Let's look at each one.

Point #1: Developing a Proof of Concept

In the DotNetInvoice case study above, I used a VA to short-circuit my product development time so we could begin to prove out the product's concept with much less effort than if we had built everything in code.

As I've automated pieces of my businesses, I've noticed an interesting trend: nearly anything I try to automate is easier to outsource first, and then automate down the line once the volume warrants it.

The reason for this is that at any given time you're likely to have, say 30 tasks on your plate, and you should be trying to remove as many as possible from your task list; both one-time and ongoing tasks.

Out of 30 tasks you might be able to outsource 6 or 8 of them *tomorrow* if you spend 2-3 hours today writing up the processes. Compare that with automation, which can take a week or more to get each task off your plate since it takes a lot of code to automate a task.

As a startup, one of your advantages is that you move very quickly. You can roll out new features much quicker than your competition. And being able to manually process some parts of a task can often reduce your development time by 50-80% which allows you to get the feature out the door and in front of customers.

If customers decide to use it, then you can automate it. If not, you can throw what little time you spent on it away. You develop the minimum required functionality to make the bare bones feature work; nothing more. You scaffold the rest with a human being; your VA.

Then, as needed, you improve the back-end automation iteratively.

Your startup time plummets to near zero even though your maintenance costs are a bit higher since you're paying someone an hourly rate to handle the task.

But that's ok, because every task you outsource to someone making $6/hour is a task that frees you up to develop new features and focus on marketing...things that make you a lot more than $6/hour.

In addition, outsourcing provides you with a written process for the task that serves as a blueprint if the time comes later to automate it.

Point #2: After Your Product Launch

The next most important time to use a VA is once your product has launched and you need to begin supporting customers.

Customers make it necessary to put processes in place for marketing, sales, support, and back-end administrative tasks. Any ongoing work that can be described in a written process can be outsourced to a VA and save incredible amounts of time for the founders.

If you do not outsource these tasks, they will get in the way of work that's truly productive for your business.

While most entrepreneurs feel like they need to keep the reins on level 1 email support, level 1 sales questions, manning the live chat window on your website, directory submissions, minor HTML tweaks, keyword research, link building, following up on canceled subscriptions, and running month-end reports...getting these tasks into the hands of a competent VA frees up vast amounts of time that can be spent growing your business.

And the cost is negligible.

Don't fall into the trap of needing to handle everything yourself. You are now an entrepreneur.

Case Studies

Here are three case studies to give you an idea of how you might use a VA in your own startup, whether serving a core business function or as administrative support.

Case Study #1: Market Research

In 2009, I launched the Micropreneur Academy. For the launch event I wanted to contact several bloggers in the startup and microISV space. I have a list of blogs that I read and quickly added them to my list to send a personal, targeted email to each. I receive enough pitches each month to know that sending a mass email to bloggers doesn't work.

In the back of my mind, I knew there were other startups/microISV blogs out there that I don't read, but I didn't want to spend the time to track them down. More importantly, I didn't want to spend the time trying to find their contact information. Enter my VA.

I tasked my VA with finding blogs that deal with startups/microISVs and rank in the top 100k in Technorati. The deliverable was a Google spreadsheet containing the blog URL, blogger's name and blogger's email.

The final spreadsheet contained 28 blogs. It was up to me to go through each one and become familiar with their content, determine its relevance to my message, and craft a targeted and personal email. Many blogs dropped off the list after a quick glance, but in the end the time saved by delegating this research task to a VA was well-worth my $12.

Case Study #2: JustBeachTowels.com

JustBeachTowels.com was an e-commerce site I purchased with hopes of a high level of automation.

The problem is that beach towel dropshippers are not the most high tech businesses, and none of them offered any kind of API for order placement. All orders had to be manually placed through their web-based shopping carts.

In the early days, I planned to build a screen scraper to pull orders from my database and automatically place them with the four dropshippers I used, but realized the level of effort and QA that would be required for this were substantial and the resulting interface would be brittle due to the screen scraping.

Instead, I assigned a VA to place all of the incoming orders. I never revisited automation due to the lack of ROI on the time it would have taken to build the screen scraping interface.

Running the site using a VA instead of automation saved me time in the long run, as I would never have made back my initial time investment on the 50+ hours required to fully automate the order placement process.

Case Study #3: ApprenticeLinemanJobs.com

Apprentice Lineman Jobs (ALJ) is a niche job website for *lineman*; electricians who work on power lines.

ALJ has a good niche and is a profitable site. But the process of scouring the internet for lineman jobs that aren't on the major job boards is a technical undertaking. Even using open source spiders, the parsing of custom web pages from dozens of job boards and company websites, then filtering out duplicates, irrelevant and junk postings is a challenging task in code.

But for a human it's pretty simple. Enter my VA.

I pay $60-100 each month to keep my job board populated with targeted, well filtered job listings you would have to scour the internet to find. The value proposition is easy – ALJ is a data aggregator and job seekers pay to save themselves the time of scouring the 200+ websites we monitor each month.

Without a VA, proving out the concept of this job board would have been impossible, and would have instead required hundreds of hours of coding just to find out if the concept would fly.

Easing Into a VA

Outsourcing is a learned skill, just like writing code. If you rush into it too quickly, you'll wind up disappointed with the results. This is most often due to the fact that you don't yet know how to work with a VA.

One of the plusses of having a VA is that you can ease into them over the course of several months. Since utilizing a VA is a learned skill, you are best to start slowly by finding someone who will work on individual tasks, then move to part-time if needed, and finally to full-time.

These hiring arrangements are described below:

- **Task-based** – ($3-10/hour overseas, $12-50/hour in the U.S.) You assign your VA an individual task and give them a deadline and maximum time to spend on the task. Since your VA works for other clients, they are in charge of prioritizing all of the tasks they receive. Task-based VA's are a great starting point to learn the ropes of delegating.
- **Part-time** – ($2-7/hour overseas, $10-$40/hour in the U.S.) Part-time VA's are dedicated to you for a certain portion of their week (typically 10, 20 or 30 hours). Part-time VA's are cheaper by the hour than task-based VAs, but you need enough work and experience to keep them busy during the time you are paying for.
- **Full-time** – ($1-$5/hour overseas, $8-35/hour in the U.S.) As you might imagine, a full-time VA is a lot of responsibility. While offering the lowest hourly rates, you need 160+ hours of work to keep them busy. If your VA is self-managing, you can lay out tasks a month at a time. If they need supervision, it's probably not worth bringing them on full-time.

The Steps

The key to learning how to work with a VA is experience. The question is: how can you get started easily and with little risk? The steps are:

1. Find a VA
2. Start with a single task and gradually increase the amount of work as you gain comfort
3. If things don't work out, find a new VA

When I began outsourcing three years ago I found that when I received the finished product I was elated that I hadn't spent 3-4 hours doing it. This made me realize how many other tasks I was able to accomplish during that time frame.

Step1: Finding a VA

I've had the best results hiring VA's in the Philippines. This is not to say that the U.S., India, Bangladesh or other countries do not have quality VA's, but the Filipinos learn English in school, do not tend to be entrepreneurial (thus are less likely to steal ideas), and are culturally service-oriented.

You may find another country to be more compatible with your management style, but after working with 10+ VA's, I now work almost exclusively with Filipinos. The main exceptions are my audio and video editors in the U.S. and Canada.

In my experience, you will be best off with one of a few choices when looking for a VA:

1. **Task-based VAs**
   o Search ODesk[73] under Admin Support -> Personal Assistant or Other.
   o Search Google for "virtual assistants." Typically the best looking websites are the firms that have their act together.
   o Search Elance[74] under Admin Support -> Admin Assistant.
2. **Part-time VAs**
   o Search ODesk under Admin Support -> Personal Assistant or Other.
   o Search Google for "part-time virtual assistants"
3. **Full-time VAs**
   o Search ODesk under Admin Support -> Personal Assistant or Other.
   o Search Google for "full-time virtual assistants"

I've had positive results and have personally hired a VA using every method listed above.

---

[73] www.odesk.com

[74] www.elance.com

My current favorite is ODesk.com. I've had exceptional luck with oDesk, and their project management tools are helpful in making sure your VA is working on your tasks. Their time clock takes screen shots of the VAs screen at random intervals so you can see the task they are performing.

A Note: Solo vs. Team
Many VA's work in teams, whether under the umbrella of a single company, or in a loose affiliation.

Solo VA's tend to be cheaper than team or larger firms.

For recurring work that's critical to your business, it's nice to work with a team. You will typically have a primary VA but when he's on vacation his replacement will step in.

For ongoing work that's not terribly time-sensitive, I've found solo VA's work out well.

When getting started, my advice is to stick with a larger VA firm. You will pay a little more but you will have more reliability, higher security and will be able to easily find a replacement when you need one.

How to Evaluate a Potential VA
My first piece of advice is to avoid spending too much time worrying about screening your VA before you hire them. In the end, how well they work out depends entirely on how well they accomplish their tasks.

In other words, reliability and the ability to understand your instructions and ask good questions are the key factors. Without hiring someone you can't get an idea about their reliability; only about their ability to understand and ask questions.

To do that, you need to evaluate their written English (or whatever language you will be working in). This includes hiring

U.S.-based VAs; competent written English skills are not a given even for native speakers.

If you're looking for general help, the only noticeable difference between the 10 VA's you are screening is their hourly rate and their ability to speak and write English.

If you need specialized work performed, you may have an additional requirement that they also know how to edit audio, for example. In that case, ask for samples of past work and experience doing the exact task you will have them to do.

The best way I've found to evaluate English skills is to email back and forth a few times, asking 2-3 basic interview questions. This will be a good indication of how well they will be able to understand your instructions, and their responses are a good indicator of how well you will be able to understand their questions. The best approach is to email with 3-5 VA's at once to speed up the process.

If you're working with a VA firm, I recommend requesting someone with excellent written English, and performing the step above with that person. If they don't live up to your standards, request a new VA and repeat the process.

In the past I've asked for writing samples but this has failed me. The problem with asking for writing samples is a VA can easily send something that's been heavily edited, or a piece written by someone else. During an email exchange you can be certain that you're catching a true glimpse of their English abilities.

Step 2: The First Task
Properly utilizing a VA is a learned skill. Very few developers will do it right the first time, which leads many who try it to give up after the first attempt. To keep you from falling into this trap, we're going to look at the best way to delegate, describe and limit tasks in the section below.

After determining your VA has solid English skills, the next step is to send them your first task. You *should* be able to tell after one task if they are going to work out.

If you've never worked with a VA, you should assume they are not technically minded. They will have basic computing skills but are nowhere near techies, so you have to prepare instructions for them as if they were your mom or dad (or at least my mom or dad).

The following is unlikely to work:

> *Open a command prompt and type 'ipconfig'*

But this should:

> *In your start menu go to the Run menu, type 'cmd' and hit enter. Once the window opens type ipconfig and hit enter.*

With that in mind, here is how I suggest you assign your first task:

- **Back everything up** before you let them touch production files. It's unlikely they will be malicious, but they might accidentally break something.
- **Provide detailed instructions** in bulleted/numbered format.
- **Screenshots help enormously**. Screencasts are even better. I record multiple screencasts each month for my VAs. Jing[75] is perfect for this.
- **Timebox your requests.** As an example, let's say you have twenty blog URLs and you want your VA to find the contact information for each one (whether it's an email address or a contact page). Provide the list of URLs to your VA and indicate they should work for 1 hour and then update you on their progress. In this manner you

---

[75] www.jingproject.com

can both check if they're doing it right, and see how long it's taking them. If it's taking longer than you think it should, ask how you can help.

- **Assume they are not as fast as you are.** If 1 URL takes you 1 minute, assume it will take your VA 5 minutes at first and they will eventually get down to 3 minutes. They will never be as fast as you are. But at $4-6/hour it's hard to complain.

- **If you have a timeline, spell it out** (e.g. "I need these by tomorrow"). If not, let them know you can wait 2 days for the results. They work when we are sleeping so you'll never get anything the same day.

Step 3: If Things Don't Work Out, Find a New VA

Finding a VA is about trial and error. I've worked through more than 6 VA's to find the folks I work with today. It's a similar process when finding a designer, developer, or any outsourcing partner. You can only tell so much from a resume; the best way to evaluate is to try them out, and this means if they don't work out you should make the decision quickly to find someone new.

It's critical that you feel comfortable with the person you're working with. It's better to cut someone loose early in the relationship before you've trained them on the inner workings of your business.

If you're working with a VA firm it's easy: simply ask for a new VA and if you can, give a specific reason why the first one did not work out.

If you're using an individual, head back to your stack of candidates from Elance, Google or ODesk. The odds are low that you will find someone great on your first try. But finding someone great will make a huge difference in the success of your outsourcing effort.

Chapter 7

Grow It or Start Over

You've launched! Congratulations. You are one of the few founders who will ever make it this far.

So what happens next?

Your answer depends entirely on your goals and personality. Once your product is out the door and real customers are using it, a startup founder is typically drawn to one of two options:

- **Grow it** – If your startup is your grand idea and you want to watch it grow over the next twenty years, then buckle down and turn it into a real business. Right now you have a product that sells; what are your next steps?
- **Start Over** – Some entrepreneurs love building and launching, but the thought of sticking with something long-term sounds hopelessly boring. That's ok; there are ways to sell or automate your startup so you can move on to your next big idea.

We'll discuss both options in this chapter.

Option 1: Grow It

Most startups that achieve early success find themselves in *the chasm*. That place Geoffrey Moore talks about in his seminal work *Crossing the Chasm*[76], where early adopters are using your product and you are trying to solve the puzzle to get to mass adoption.

Not surprisingly, by the time the chasm is in sight you will know more about your customers than you ever thought possible. No book, blog or conference could ever teach you more about your customers than you learn from watching them use your software.

With customer knowledge happening organically, the most important learning you will do during this time will come from your peers. These are the software and web startup founders in other industries who have made it, and share their knowledge through books, blogs, podcasts, presentations, and online communities.

What follows are the best ways to interact with and learn from your startup peers, both in person and online, locally and worldwide:

Conferences
- **Business of Software** (businessofsoftware.org) – The premier conference for "real" software companies. One of the best software startup networking opportunities I've found.
- **LessConf** (lessconf.lesseverything.com) – Relatively inexpensive, LessConf covers everything from "startups to design to marketing to business."
- **Future of Web Apps** (futureofwebapps.com) – A worldwide conference for web developers and entrepreneurs.

---

[76] http://tinyurl.com/2cj2sh8

Meetups

- **Meetup.com** (www.meetup.com) – In nearly every city you'll find meetups with other entrepreneurs, startup founders and techies. The best source for monthly networking.

- **StartupDigest** (thestartupdigest.com) – Though more geared towards venture-backed startups, the startup digest caters to 36 cities around the world, and provides a weekly update of startup events in your area.

Blogs

- **OnStartups** (onstartups.com) – Dharmesh Shah has owned multiple successful companies, raised venture capital, and he shares his insights on this, one of the best startup blogs.

- **MicroISV on a Shoestring** (www.kalzumeus.com) – Brilliant Micropreneur Patrick McKenzie shares every last detail about his microISV.

- **A Smart Bear** (blog.asmartbear.com) – Jason Cohen grew and sold his software company. Now he gives back to the startup community by sharing his knowledge here.

- **Steve Blank** (steveblank.com) – Steve Blank is a Silicon Valley veteran, but many of his insights apply to self-funded startups.

- **Lessons Learned** (www.startuplessonslearned.com) – Eric Ries' Lean Startup Methodology closely parallels the Micropreneur Methodology I've laid out in this book, and his knowledge of the startup process is unparalleled.

- **Single Founder** (www.singlefounder.com) – Mike Taber shares his insight and wisdom from 10 years in the entrepreneurial trenches.

- **Paul Graham** (www.paulgraham.com/articles.html) – Though venture-focused, Graham's insights into the startup process are unique and powerful.

- **Software by Rob** (www.softwarebyrob.com) – My blog, where I talk about all things self-funded.

Online Communities

- **The Micropreneur Academy** (www.micropreneur.com) – A paid membership community of bootstrappers and Micropreneurs, brought together to learn, be accountable, share community, and launch successful startups.
- **Answers.OnStartups** (answers.onstartups.com) – A question and answer community geared specifically towards startups.
- **StartupToDo.com** (www.startuptodo.com) – A productivity application for startup founders built by Bob Walsh.
- **Business of Software Forums** (discuss.joelonsoftware.com/?biz) – A forum frequented by the microISV crowd.

Podcasts

- **Mixergy** (mixergy.com) – Revealing interviews with successful entrepreneurs. The host (Andrew Warner) is one of the best I've seen at getting to the bottom of a founder's success.
- **Startups for the Rest of Us** (www.startupsfortherestofus.com) – A podcast hosted by Mike Taber and myself that looks at specific tactics for starting, launching and growing a self-funded startup
- **The Web 2.0 Show** (web20show.com) – A show that interviews founders of self-funded and venture-backed web startups.
- **37signals Podcast** (37signals.com/podcast) – Wit, wisdom and cynicism from the outspoken founders of 37signals.
- **The Startup Success Podcast** (startuppodcast.wordpress.com) – A long-running interview podcast for self-funded startups.

Option 2: Starting Over

To some, the idea of starting over is invigorating. For these intrepid founders, running the same startup for 10 years is akin to writing SQL reports in a windowless cubicle. Why work on the same, boring thing when you can try something new?

But before you can make the switch, you need to find closure for your existing startup. The two most common approaches are to automate it or sell it.

We'll discuss both in this section.

Option 1: Automate It

Given the low valuations of software products and web applications (which we'll discuss in the next section), the option to automate your startup tends to be the best approach. You spent months building your application and bringing it to market – if it's profitable and you spend no time on it, why sell?

Typically, a bootstrapper will not follow the path of automation. They will sell or grow a startup, so I'm going to use the term "Micropreneur" for the remainder of this section.

Serial vs. Parallel Micropreneurship

The terms serial and parallel can be a bit confusing so let's examine them briefly.

- *Serial* implies "one after another"
- *Parallel* implies "at the same time"

You may have heard the term serial entrepreneur floating around the business press. This is typically used to describe someone who starts a startup, grows it, sells it, and moves on to the next one.

Marc Andreessen was a co-founder of Netscape, followed by Opsware, Ning, and now a venture capital fund. He is a good example of this, as are Jeff Hawkins and Donna Dubinsky, founders of Palm, Handspring and now Numenta.

But the challenge as a startup entrepreneur is that you can't start two companies at once. Starting a company requires enormous amounts of effort and time, and can't be done in parallel. There's no other way but to start one, sell it or close it down, then move on to the next.

Micropreneurship is different. With Micropreneurship you *can* run multiple companies at once, albeit tiny companies. So why don't we call this concept Parallel Micropreneurship?

The effort of any Micropreneur product is front-loaded. The effort put into building the product and automating marketing, support, etc... are huge unpaid up-front time investments. But once they are complete you will have a business that requires a small amount of monthly maintenance compared to the income it generates.

Once automation is in place it's almost as if the first product falls off your radar and you are freed up to start another. And you can do this without selling or closing it down.

So a parallel entrepreneur would be insane (who would think it's sane to run two businesses at the same time)? And the same goes for Micropreneurs (you don't want to try to launch and ramp-up two Micropreneur businesses at the same time).

But doing things one after another (in serial) actually works. It just so happens that in entrepreneurship you have to launch then sell or close down a business to start your next one. With Micropreneurship you don't; you can keep it running *in the background* while you launch your next product.

Section 1: The Advantages of Multiple Products
You may question the concept of owning multiple products at once. Why would you put yourself through the hassle?

Advantage #1: The Ability to Choose Small Niches

With a traditional business you have to choose a market that has the potential to generate a substantial payout each month. Unless you want to remain at your day job, you'll need to make enough money every month to cover all of your expenses. This means that attacking something like creating Scavenger Hunt maps is not a good idea as the market is unlikely to ever generate a full-time income.

With the ability to attack niches that can provide $500-$2000/month in income, you are able to fly under the radar of most businesses. Even small software companies won't attack markets this small, which means it's easier to own a substantial piece, if not all, of the market.

Having a $2000/month niche to yourself is much better than having a 20% market share of a $10,000/month niche. No competition means lower ad rates, less SEO competition, and as the market grows your income will automatically increase since you own the entire market.

Advantage #2: Income Diversification

Being self-employed is risky business, but it's even riskier if you own a single product. Imagine if your entire income is tied up in your trusty Scavenger Hunt designer software and 37signals releases a version of this software tomorrow? Or Google updates its algorithm and accidentally drops you from its index?

You're going to see a huge drop in income.

By having a *product portfolio* (a collection of products owned by a Serial Micropreneur) you diversify your income, and thus diversify your risk. If any one product fails or has a drop in income, it's likely your other products can make up the slack. Or at least keep you going until you can fix things.

For me, my consumer-focused products stayed level during the recession and kept me from having to take on consulting work to pay the bills.

Advantage #3: Attention Diversification

Another part of diversification is it allows you to try new ideas over time to see what works. Most of us are creative people and have tons of product ideas floating around in our heads. It's a real bummer to have to commit to one idea for two, three or five years.

Knowing you can try one idea but move on to another in 6 months to a year once you get it automated frees you up to take more risks than if you have to decide which product you're going to own for the next 10 years. There's a big difference in mindset there and it allows you to make riskier decisions. If an idea doesn't work out, scrap it and start another one.

In addition, I find it more interesting on a day to day basis to work on multiple products. When I get bored of one I focus on another. It keeps me motivated and entertained to have a variety of challenges.

Advantage #4: Economies of Scale

Setting up an issue tracker, tech support system, forums, documentation templates, support email templates, screencasting software, microphone, and all the other necessities you need to support a product requires an initial time investment.

Not surprisingly, the second time around it takes about one-third the time. Not only do you already have systems in place, but you can use the same software for multiple products and there's no up-front learning curve to learn how to record a screencast or setup an autoresponder. You've done it before and that translates into a lower time and money investment per product than if you have only one.

Advantage #5: You Can Focus on What You Enjoy

Perhaps you enjoy the idea phase; the time when you brainstorm tons of ideas and research each one, narrowing down to your final choice.

Or perhaps it's the startup phase where you're writing a ton of code, building new features and preparing for launch.

Or maybe it's marketing. Drawing people to your site for the first time and seeing those first dollars roll into your bank account.

If you own one product, you will do each of these things once. You will never brainstorm niches, write green field code, or launch a new product again.

If these aspects of product development are what you enjoy most, Serial Micropreneurship is the way to be able to experience them multiple times.

Advantage #6: Experience Transfers

Finding a niche, launching, setting up AdWords and SEO, email marketing, support...the more knowledge you gain in each of these areas the better *all* of your products become.

The first time I built a mailing list, it instantly occurred to me that I needed to build mailing lists for all of my products. These tools scale infinitely; once you learn how to wield one, it can be applied to every product you launch, whether you own a consulting firm, an e-commerce site, a software product or an ebook.

Experience holds up and will earn you much more money if you can leverage it across multiple products.

Section 2: The Pitfalls of Multiple Products

Pitfall #1: Task Switching

The biggest downside to owning multiple products is the task switching. There's no doubt about it – switching tasks is not efficient. You will be more efficient if you have only a single product on which to focus all of your energy.

However, if you are organized, plan effectively, and time box well, you can reduce the inefficiency you will experience.

Pitfall #2: Outsourcing and Automation are Crucial

If you are not willing to outsource and automate *extensively*, do not consider being a Serial Micropreneur. If you need to make every code change or answer every incoming email, you will not survive running multiple products. The workload is too large.

This is not a pitfall as much as a stern warning. Do not build or buy your second product until you have outsourced or automated as much as you possibly can with your first product. Only when you begin to feel like you have a lot of free time while your first product continues to generate revenue should you consider making the move to Serial Micropreneurship.

Section 3: The Formula

Here is the formula for Serial Micropreneurship:

1. Build or buy a product
2. Launch or revamp it
3. Grow revenue to its natural plateau
4. Outsource and automate ruthlessly
5. Go to step 1

From this, we can answer a few questions about Serial Micropreneurship.

Question #1: When Should I Put a Product on Auto-Pilot?

With every product I owned I found a natural plateau to earning levels. With basic marketing in place and automated, your product will bring in X dollars per month, give or take 20%. Breaking through that plateau requires a substantial time investment; it often means moving into an entirely new market.

Ultimately it's up to how you feel about the product: when it hits a plateau, do you have the momentum to push it through?

Two years ago, when DotNetInvoice hit its first earnings plateau, I put it on auto-pilot, purchased several products and revamped them. This was a great learning experience, and turned out to be profitable. In addition, it re-charged my batteries and created some desire to come back to DotNetInvoice. Recently I've come all the way back around now that I have the momentum to make another big push and hopefully break through into the next earnings level.

Then, it will go back on autopilot until the next round.

Question #2: How Do I Keep Maintenance to a Minimum?
Once your product is built and launched there are three areas that will require ongoing maintenance:

- Support
- New Features
- Marketing

Support
If you can hone your email response snippets, optimize your installation process and online help docs, and especially if you own a SaaS app, you can minimize your support time. Every time you receive a support request, your first thought should be "how can I make sure I never receive this question again." You will make a time investment beyond a simple reply, but it will pay for itself for years to come.

Also with support, depending on your product, it's likely you will be able to hire a domestic VA to handle your front-line email support. You will pay more for someone in your own country, but they will be fluent in your language and better able to provide higher-quality support.

I outsource 30-40 hours per month of email support to VA's, which means I can work one less day per week, or work on one or two more products per month.

New Features
If your product is on auto-pilot, you should always fix bugs in a timely manner but you may or may not want to develop new features.

If your product is selling consistently at the plateau income level and you are not investing development time, it's hard to justify working on new features when you could be building a new product. If your product is desired by the market as it stands, why continue to invest development hours *unless that's what you want to do.* It really is about doing what you want.

If you have competition, it's more difficult. This is one reason I talked in chapter 2 about entering niche markets with little competition. This allows you to put a product on auto-pilot for longer periods of time.

Let me be clear about one thing: *no product is going to sell at the same level forever.* It's going to need updates at some point. But the goal is to build a bunch of new features at once, invest a lot of time into the product, and then move on to your next product while this one brings in money on auto-pilot. You can return to it 4, 8 or 12 months down the road to continue improvements as needed.

Marketing
The final piece is marketing. Putting marketing on auto-pilot is a lot easier than you might think.

Remember that marketing is about bringing people to your website, and converting them to customers.

For conversions, once you've invested time up front to improve your conversion rates, your site will continue to convert at this level until something in the market changes. A high converting page doesn't just stop converting...it continues to convert at that rate for a long time.

So that leaves traffic. Let's look at the most popular sources of traffic:

- **PPC Ads** – Ad campaigns require an initial investment and then a tiny amount of weekly or even monthly maintenance. Once you've found keywords that convert and ads that work, you only have to adjust as your competition changes. I have campaigns that have been running with minor tweaks for more than two years. The time investment was in the first 2-3 months testing ads and finding the keywords that converted.
- **SEO** – Once SEO is in place, it's all about maintenance. If you monitor your traffic using Google Analytics and compare month over month you'll notice when there's a decline for a specific keyword and you can investigate. Otherwise, SEO is also an up-front investment.
- **Incoming Links** – Similar to PPC and SEO, once you have incoming links, the traffic basically trickles in each month. Nothing to do here.

While it is true that to grow a business you have to invest time, that's not what we're discussing here. We're talking about being able to put a business on hibernate for a period of time, be it a month or six months, and have it maintain its income level with minimal maintenance.

This is the real secret to leveraging a product to live the lifestyle of your choice. This is Serial Micropreneurship.

Option 2: Sell It
If automation doesn't work out, selling your product is a good fall-back plan. The first thing to realize is that you're not going to get as much as you feel that it's worth.

First Things First: Profit

If your startup does not turn a profit, the odds of making an exit for anything more than a few thousand dollars is remote. Forget the image of unprofitable YouTube selling to Google for $1.65 billion...that doesn't happen unless you have millions of users and exponential growth.

How Are Software Products Valued?

There are people who've spent their entire careers doing nothing but learning how to value a business. Laundromats, as an example, are typically valued at around 50 times their monthly net profit (with adjustments made for the age of the equipment, length remaining on your lease, and a slew of other factors).

Like every kind of business, websites and small software products have their own formula. If you spend any length of time on the website marketplaces, you'll learn a rule of thumb: a website or domain name typically sells for between 6 and 24 months of net profit. But 12 months is a reasonable starting point.

Keep in mind there are many adjustments to that number. If you have a generic parked domain name that gets a lot of type in traffic you can garner 24-36 months of profit, or a particularly high earning website that's well automated can bring 20-24 months. Websites that require a substantial amount of ongoing work can go as low as 2x or 3x monthly profit.

Those are the numbers for websites, which tend to have a lot of potential buyers because a lot of people have the skills to maintain them.

Software products, on the other hand, are a bit harder to sell because you tend to be limited to software developers who know the language in which the product is written. So realize that starting out, your potential market is smaller and thus your valuation will be in the lower end of that range.

Add to that the ongoing maintenance and support a software product requires and you'll see why valuations for true software products typically run from 6-15 months. Products like AdSense websites and EBooks require virtually zero maintenance and support.

But I Thought Our Startup Would be Worth Millions!
Unless your startup is bringing in six figures of annual profit, the dream of selling for millions is...well, a dream.

Whatever ideas the business press has placed in your head; please check them at the door. They write stories more to sell magazines than to educate you on what happens to the vast majority of businesses that are sold each year.

The reality of selling a small software product or website is that valuations are based on multiples of profit with only rare exceptions granting additional money for exceptional web design or an exceptionally unique application idea.

Realistically, startups are much better bought than sold. Meaning, if someone approaches you with an offer to purchase your startup, you should be able to ask for a higher price than if you sold your startup on the open market.

This backwards logic applies because if someone has approached you, they have a unique desire for your application, which will likely motivate them to move beyond simple profit multiples.

With this knowledge in hand, I advise startup founders looking for an exit to attempt to automate their startup first, and only when they are unable to do so, consider a sale.

What We Can Learn From Valuations

Since valuations are highly correlated with profit, increasing your profit *will increase your valuation.*

The other factor that impacts valuation is how much time is required each month to maintain your product. If you have a website whose sole income is through consulting work, your valuation will be very low...it could easily be 2-3x monthly profit, due to the time intensity of performing consulting work.

From these thoughts we realize that the open market places value on profit and automation much more than technical capabilities, features, raw traffic without revenue, or web design.

Thus, the key to increasing your product's value in the eyes of the market is to optimize profit, through marketing and sales, and minimize the ongoing time investment through outsourcing and automation.

The interesting thing is the more you focus on these "exit strategy" tactics, the more efficient your business becomes.

Think about it, the more you increase revenue and reduce your required time investment, the better your business becomes for you...today. In other words, the goals of the market and the goals you should be striving for today are very much in line with each other.

Think Like a Potential Buyer

It's enlightening to look at your product as a potential buyer. You can imagine the questions someone would ask if they were acquiring your product. Working out the answers to those questions in advance will increase confidence and the price someone is willing to pay in the future should you ever decide to sell.

The Lesson Is: Track Everything

Even if you never plan to sell your startup, you should be collecting and reviewing the data that will ultimately allow you to facilitate an easy sale.

You need to know this information to understand and improve your product, so use this as impetus to start tracking it in case the day ever comes where you need to sell.

Here are key metrics you should track:

- **Traffic Stats** – I recommend using Google Analytics.
- **Revenue and Expenses** – Spend 30 minutes at the end of every month going through your payment processing, PayPal and credit card statements and determine your total income and expenditures for this product to calculate your profit for the month. You'll be surprised at how quickly little expenses add up.
- **Monitor Your Domain and Business Names** – Potential buyers will Google your product name, domain name, and business names to see if the product has a good or bad reputation. Head these off early using Google Alerts[77].
- **Track Hours Spent** – Using a tool like SlimTimer[78], track every minute you spend working on your product, broken down into development, support and marketing. This allows you to monetize your time during month-end, and to speak honestly about the monthly time investment if you sell. In my experience, the number of hours you spend on a product is less than it "feels."
- **Hosting** – Make sure your product doesn't share a database with another website. Keep things separate so it can be easily migrated to another server.

---

[77] www.google.com/alerts/

[78] www.slimtimer.com

- **Licensing** – Keep your legal house in order. Don't use open source or third-party code that could raise licensing issues down the line. You may get away with it now, but when you try to sell your product you will regret it.

A Case Study for Increasing Product Value

CMS Themer[79] is a theming service for designers. A customer submits a website design as a PSD file, and CMS Themer returns a content management system (CMS) theme within 5 business days. The most popular CMS's are WordPress, Drupal and Joomla.

When the site was originally offered for sale by the previous owner, he had essentially limited the sale to someone with theming skills, and someone who was able to devote 5-15 hours per week building themes. This instantly shrank his potential market.

But I had connections with an offshore design firm and I bought CMS Themer for a song (less than 2x monthly profit). The site paid itself off in net profit in 4 months. I owned it a total of 9 profitable months and sold it for a substantial gain.

The reason the site had literally hundreds of interested parties when I listed it for sale was due to one reason: I had outsourced the hard part of theming), and had tracked my time so was able to document that I had earned over $100/hour on time spent working on CMS Themer.

I was selling a business, and a well paying one, rather than a job like the previous owner.

---

[79] www.cmsthemer.com

If You Decide to Sell

If you decide to sell your product, your best bet is your professional network. Your first option should be to email colleagues and float it to your LinkedIn connections.

If you have a blog with decent traffic, consider announcing the sale but be careful with how much information you divulge. Don't offer up intimate product details for the search engines to eternally index, making the product less appealing to potential buyers.

When you contact colleagues about your sale, mention the following:

- **Your Price Range** – Start with the range I provided above (6-15x monthly profit).
- **Non-Disclosure Requirement** – At this point things are still private, and if you expect to sell for more than $10k, protect the future buyer by requiring an NDA before disclosing financial information.
- **Prepare Your Sales Kit** – Include a detailed summary of the product in a PDF document:
    - Product Overview
    - Customers
    - Technical details
    - Positive reviews and high-profile links
    - Revenue
    - Expenses
    - Partnerships
    - Personnel
    - Competition
    - Website traffic (although include a detailed traffic report in a separate document)
    - Assets included in the sale
    - Price range
    - Future plans (surely you will have a list a mile long)

- o Non-compete – Mention whether you are willing to sign a non-compete in this space.
- **Transferring Assets** – If the sale is over $1,000 indicate you would prefer to use escrow.com and split fees. Escrow.com facilitates the exchange of your product once funds are deposited in an escrow account. Your other option is to use a sales contract that specifies the following: half of the purchase price to be paid up-front (via check), the assets are transferred, and then the second half is paid. If the purchase price is less than $1,000, opt for a simple PayPal transaction.

Give your network time to mull it over and pass things around. Rushing the sale is a sign of desperation and will decrease the chance that you will get a fair price.

If you are unable to find a buyer within your network, you can either attempt to automate your startup (which I recommend), or sell your product at auction. The eBay of website and software sales is Flippa[80].

Conclusion
Automating your startup should be your first choice. But if you are unable or unwilling to do so, getting a lump-sum payment through a sale can be an appealing option.

---

[80] www.flippa.com

The Postlude

The Grand Finale

I began this book with the following statement:

> *If you aren't frantically underlining, highlighting or taking notes as you read each chapter, then I have not achieved my goal for this book.*

I welcome your comments to that end. Contact me anytime at rob@softwarebyrob.com.

To ask a question, make a comment or purchase the print, ebook or audio version of this book, visit www.StartupBook.net

Until next time.

A Final Note about the Micropreneur Academy

With my colleague Mike Taber, I run an online startup community called the Micropreneur Academy (www.Micropreneur.com).

The Micropreneur Academy is a paid online learning environment and community website for startup founders.

Although this book contains a small amount of material from the Micropreneur Academy, it only covers topics that are conducive to the printed page.

The purpose of the Micropreneur Academy is to present topics that require interactive elements (screencasts, audio, and worksheets), topics that change frequently, cutting-edge approaches and our complete Rolodex of vendors and contractors. In addition it provides a community of like-minded startup founders accessible via private forums.

If you are interested in launching or growing your startup faster, as an owner of this book you are entitled to the first month of the Academy at no charge. To receive your free month visit www.Micropreneur.com/book/

Made in the USA
Lexington, KY
04 August 2014